Billy Kim's witness to Jesus Christ has made a life-changing difference in Korea, America, and the world. His family's hardships during and after the Korean War, his remarkable journey to the United States, his bittersweet relationship with Bob Jones University, his heartwarming romance with his wife, Trudy, his unmistakable call to evangelism, his dynamic partnership with Billy Graham, his radio outreach to closed countries, and his gospel influence on world leaders—all these make his life a memorable and inspirational story of God's abundant grace.

PHILIP RYKEN
President
Wheaton College

It would be no exaggeration to say that Billy Kim is one of the more remarkable Christian leaders I have come to know. I have watched him engage with presidents and pastors, the poor and the affluent, his family and even my own children. He is as natural speaking before tens of thousands as he is talking with a stranger. His gifts of encouragement, inspiration, and sharing Jesus know no bounds. Dr. Kim's life story is one of the most powerful testimonies of God's grace in this generation. If you want to understand the grace of God in and through one of His faithful followers, you have to read this book.

BARRY H. COREY
President
Biola University

It is with joy that I commend the Billy Kim story! What a wonderful confirmation of the biblical witness that when I am weak then I am strong. This book is a testimony of how, when one is completely dedicated to Christ, He will bless you. It is the story of how a young Korean houseboy became a great evangelist and also president of the Baptist World Alliance, representing the community of 150 million Baptists worldwide! Read this book and you will be blessed!

DENTON LOTZ
General Secretary emeritus
Baptist World Alliance

The life of Reverend Kim is a living history and testimony of perseverance and courage. Teeming with invaluable life lessons and a stirring narrative, *The Life of Billy Kim* guides us on a remarkable man's journey to find God and the unexpected blessings we find in tenacity and faith. I recommend this beautiful autobiogr~~~~~ ~~ ~~~~~~~~ ud to call a dear friend.

CHARLES B. RANGEL
US Congressman (New York)

D1411899

THE LIFE OF BILLY KIM

FROM HOUSEBOY
TO WORLD EVANGELIST

THE LIFE OF BILLY KIM

FROM HOUSEBOY
TO WORLD EVANGELIST

BILLY KIM

MOODY PUBLISHERS

CHICAGO

Korean edition: Translated by Sumi Lamb, edited by Larry Nickels
Moody Publishers editor: Jim Vincent
Interior design: Ragont Design
Cover design: Dean Renninger
Cover image: Billy Kim (right) translating message by Billy Graham at Seoul '73 Crusade. Courtesy of Billy Graham Evangelistic Association. Used with permission. All rights reserved.

Library of Congress Cataloging-in-Publication Data

Kim, Jang-hwan, 1934-
The life of Billy Kim : from houseboy to world evangelist / Billy Kim.
    pages cm
Includes bibliographical references.
1. Kim, Jang-hwan, 1934- 2. Evangelists—Korea (South)—Biography. I. Title.
BV3785.K55A3 2015
269'.2092—dc23
[B]
                          2014034370

                    ISBN: 978-0-8024-1263-8

We hope you enjoy this book from Moody Publishers. Our goal is to provide high-quality, thought-provoking books and products that connect truth to your real needs and challenges. For more information on other books and products written and produced from a biblical perspective, go to www.moodypublishers.com or write to:

Moody Publishers
820 N. LaSalle Boulevard
Chicago, IL 60610

3 5 7 9 10 8 6 4 2

Printed in the United States of America

CONTENTS

A WORD OF APPRECIATION

BILLY GRAHAM

Billy Kim is a fellow evangelist and my personal friend. His alertness, faithfulness to the gospel of Christ, and his availability to serve, inspire everyone who makes his acquaintance. I value the good fellowship we enjoyed in Korea and appreciated him as my interpreter and co-laborer in the gospel.

Billy Kim's story is the story of what God can do through the life of a person who is committed to His will. Your background may be different from Billy Kim's, but his experience of God's faithfulness can teach us all about the ways God leads and protects His children.

May God bless you and challenge you to a deeper dedication to Jesus Christ.

June, 1979
Montreat, NC

FOREWORD

From the early chapters of *The Life of Billy Kim*, it's evident that God has laid His hand directly on Billy's life. God dramatically chose him out of poverty and obscurity during wartime to become a tremendously influential global leader for the spread of the gospel, a humble witness and voice to the powerful and powerless alike.

At the fiftieth anniversary of the Far East Broadcasting Corporation in 2006, Billy invited me as the featured speaker for an evangelistic event held in the Seoul Olympic Stadium. There was an overflow crowd. Very few people have been given the influence to draw this size of a crowd and have such a tangible impact on the lives of millions. Billy Kim has that influence. Billy is one of the world's most effective evangelists and great organizational leaders of our day because he has used the influence God had given him to change history. It's my privilege to meet hundreds of world leaders, but few have the resolute character and respect of Billy Kim.

Billy Kim continues to serve God's purposes. His life continues to echo the words of the apostle Paul, "However, I consider my life worth nothing to me; my only aim is to finish the race and complete the task the Lord Jesus has given me—the task of testifying to the good news of God's grace" (Acts 20:24 NIV).

To know Billy is to be prayed for by Billy, to be served by Billy, and to be honored by Billy. He truly sacrifices himself for others. He is a faithful witness to the love, forgiveness, and hope of our Lord, Jesus Christ. I am thankful for the life and partnership of my dear friend Billy Kim. I love him deeply.

Billy's life story will encourage and challenge you to follow the example of seeing the God opportunities set before you—and then, out of obedience, to follow through as a servant willing to serve as God leads.

Dr. Rick Warren
Senior Pastor, Saddleback Church, Lake Forest, California
Author of *The Purpose Driven Life* and
The Purpose Driven Church

PROLOGUE
WHEN A MAN MEETS GOD
MIRACLES HAPPEN

I often tell people, "History happens when a man meets a man, and miracles happen when a man meets God!" I say this from experience. During my years as a houseboy for the United States Army, I met Sergeant Carl Powers, a soldier defending Korea during the Korean War. This led to my studying in the United States at the age of seventeen, something that before had been only a dream for me. I held in my hand a mere $130 going to America. However, this is where I met God and was born again.

History and miracles combined to make me the person I am today.

In 1959, after graduating from Bob Jones University with an MA and having been ordained as a pastor, I returned to Korea and started my ministry holding on to the words of Scripture: "For to me to live is Christ, and to die is gain" (Philippians 1:21). Since then fifty years have passed. As I reflect back, the words of a hymn come to mind: "What I am today is through the Lord's abundant grace."

Yes, who I am today is through my Lord's grace alone.

This book has become possible because of the desire of the CEO of Nachimban (Compass) Publishing Company, Yong Ho Kim, who has closely observed my ministry for the past twenty-five years. He wanted to leave an example for future generations of how God's work had been revealed through my life. This book became possible based on my interviews with Mr. Kim along with the help of Professor Jae Sung Yoo.

While I was praying for the expansion of my ministry of the gospel,

Mr. Kim was stirring up new winds in the Korean church's publications and seminars. I asked God to bless me with a partner, and He led me to Yong Ho Kim. Ever since that day, he has remained my steadfast supporter.

As he made his inaugural speech during the congress of the Far East Broadcasting Company operations committee, Mr. Kim said, "I believe Pastor Billy Kim's life is a life of 3 Es: Evangelist—a strict gospel evangelist (finding and declaring the true gospel); Economist—earning a five-talents profit (a steward); and Energizer—an energizing server." He has now published in Korea a book[1] on my life based on these three Es that characterize who I am today. *The Life of Billy Kim* is based on that book, and those three Es form the basis for the three parts of this story.

I appreciate the fine editorial work of Larry Nickels in performing the initial editing for our American publisher. I am also grateful to Sumi Lamb in translating the manuscript from the original Korean to English.

To my wife, Trudy, I give thee much love and gratitude.

I was asked to write my autobiography not because of who I am but because of how far God continues to take me. The revelations of God do not start or stop at a particular point in life but continue as long as we are receptive to His Word, the Bible. As a result, I have written this autobiography in a third-person narrative to show the story of my life not as how I experienced it, but through the eyes of God. This tale is not mine to tell, but God's.

I sincerely pray that this autobiography will bring great glory to God who has accomplished great things through His servant. In addition, I pray that this will give some guidance to future generations as they serve our Lord. Furthermore, I pray that this book becomes a guide and a vision for future Christian young people.

Above all, I praise Thee, God, with Acts 20:24: "I do not count my life of any value nor as precious to myself, if only I may finish my course and the ministry that I received from the Lord Jesus, to testify to the gospel of the grace of God."

김장환
Pastor Billy Jang Hwan Kim

Part 1

THE EVANGELIST
FINDING AND DECLARING THE GOSPEL

Had it not been for Carl Powers, a sergeant who served his country during the Korean War, I would not have had the chance of a lifetime to come to America for my education. Had it not been for a dormitory neighbor, Jerry Major, who shared the gospel with an international student who was fighting culture shock, language barriers, and severe homesickness, I would not have come to know the truth of unfathomable love embedded in the living words of John 3:16.

In part 1 we see God's desire and power to change lives when people let Him use them. Accepting Christ changed my life. Without Christ in my life, I cannot imagine ever speaking before a large crowd and witnessing the power of God to transform people. The power of God can change your life too, so you can know Him and even share the Word with people closest to you.

Evangelism can begin at home and in our surrounding communities. When we are zealous in declaring the gospel, God supplies all our needs.

INTRODUCTION
PASTOR KIM AND
PRESIDENT CASTRO

Politically, Cuba bears the marks left by the renowned Argentine revolutionist Che Guevara, a prominent communist figure in the Cuban revolution (1956–59). In Havana's old section, colonial methods have been completely preserved from Spain's prime era in the 1500s, and it is registered as a world heritage site. Havana, with its long coastal seawall, Malecón, alongside the city's picturesque scenery, is a famous vacation spot. Ernest Hemingway wrote *The Old Man and the Sea* in Havana, and a small fishing village in Havana is the setting for the novel.

On July 5, 2000, pastor and evangelist Billy Kim was in Havana to attend the inauguration of the general secretary of the Baptist World Alliance (BWA) and his own installation as the new BWA president. One year earlier he had been recommended as the succeeding president by the BWA executive committee. He was chosen because he met six criteria for the position: a person of vision for world missions, someone who has a successful ministry, someone who fervently prays, someone who is diligent to serve, a leader in bringing harmony, and a powerful preacher of the gospel.

Pastor Kim had been officially elected as president in January 2000 at the 18th Baptist World Congress held in Melbourne, Australia. He was the first Korean to be elected president. (In 1975, there had been an ethnic Hong Kong president, David Wong, but he was a US citizen.)

Now the Korean television and the press scrambled to provide detailed coverage in Cuba of Billy Kim's inauguration. In fact, the attention of the world's media and the religious community had already been on him, and on Korea. Former US president Jimmy Carter, with whom he had built a longtime friendship, had also sent a heartfelt congratulatory message stating, "Your election as president of BWA is a definite result of your long service for God."

Of the 160 million Baptist church members within the Baptist World Alliance in 2000, Americans made up 50 million of them. This included then-president Bill Clinton, Vice President Al Gore, former president Jimmy Carter, along with the head of the US Senate and the House of Representatives, and the Senate's chief of diplomacy. As such, the president of BWA would be in a position to have a significant impact upon Western societies such as the United States and Europe.

Even so, Pastor Kim pledged what had been on his mind at the inaugural ceremony: "Lord, I will use this enormous official post for the spread of the gospel." Then he made up his mind to start immediately, while there in Havana. To him, this inaugural ceremony was the starting place of his initiation to spread the gospel to a bigger world. He was more interested in the spiritual salvation of the Cuban nationals than his inauguration.

During that time, the Christian community of Cuba, including Catholics, remained frozen, the lingering effects of the communist revolution once led by the president of the Council of States, Fidel Castro. Of course, President Castro was a prime candidate for Billy's spreading of the gospel. However, this was not an easy task. He was known as being a dyed-in-the-wool communist who had never met with any other religious leader except Pope John Paul II.

On his way to Cuba, Kim had stopped by the US headquarters of the Lockman Foundation, and its president, Robert Lambeth, which had prepared a special Spanish Bible for President Castro. In spite of his tight schedule, he prayed earnestly for President Castro and the souls of Cuba.

On the day of his inauguration, Billy thought he would be able to share the gospel with President Castro at the National Capitol, where the president would speak prior to the inauguration. However, Castro's speech was cancelled due to a six-year-old boy. Elián González had lost his mother during a storm that capsized their boat headed for the United

States. Now after an international custody battle, the boy had been re-turned to his father in Cuba. President Castro would present the young boy with Cuba's highest award, and Billy would lose this opportunity to meet with Castro and present the special Bible and to share the gospel.

Later, after his installation as BWA president, Kim felt anxious that he might leave Cuba without having a chance to see Castro, so during a special reception he handed the Bible to the Cuban vice-minister of religion. President Kim asked the vice-minister to give it to President Castro.

Throughout the general convention, Baptist church representatives held more than forty evangelistic conferences in the city of Havana. And although he had given the Bible to the religious representative, Billy rose early every morning to pray for some opportunity to meet with the Cuban president. "Lord, please lead me to Castro so that I may share the gospel with him."

God did not let his prayers go in vain. As the last day of the joint conference arrived, just three hours prior to the event, Castro's associates urgently requested to see Pastor Kim. Without as much as a moment to think, Kim, BWA Secretary General Denton Lotz, and past president Nilson Fanini hurried to the presidential office where President Castro was waiting.

President Castro, in his usual trademark khaki military uniform, greeted Billy. He was a tall, seventy-four-year-old grandfather, with hints of gray in his hair, mustache, and beard. He definitely would have been a great Santa Claus if he had been wearing a red hat and coat.

As Billy was still standing, he talked with President Castro for about ten minutes, because Castro had not invited him to sit down. *He does not wish to speak to a Christian such as myself for a long time*, Billy thought. In his mind he thought that President Castro wished to send him off as soon as possible. His predictions had been surprisingly wrong.

President Castro led him to his official presidential office. The Spanish Bible had been handed back to Billy by the Cuban vice-minister of religion, and the first thing to do was to give this Spanish Bible directly to the Cuban president as a gift.

"When I was young, my mother spent a lot of time reading the Bible to me," Castro said. President Castro then opened the pages of the Bible and read a few verses from it. Billy sensed that the president really appreciated the Bible through his actions and the sparkle in his eyes. Castro then said, "I received baptism from the Catholic Church in order to prevent myself from being mistreated. . . . Luckily, I received the baptism free, which normally cost two pesos." Billy began to gain a little understanding as to why Castro had become a communist.

Then President Castro made a clearly political remark. "I hope that the United States will release the economic sanctions as soon as possible. I am deeply grateful that there has been an adoption of a resolution, to release the economic sanctions, at this Baptist World Alliance Congress." Billy now realized the reason for the urgency in wanting to meet with him.

Billy gave back the previously written message, which was to be addressed by the vice-minister of religion on behalf of President Castro. President Castro then raised his pen and personally wrote a new greeting message in Spanish. Then he said, "Through this inaugural ceremony, I have come to realize the depth of our Cuban Baptist church believers. This event has brought a good image of Christians to the Cuban people."

"I will propose active measures to the international community, to ease the economic sanctions against Cuba," Billy replied.

After they had chatted for a while, it was nearly time to start the conference for that evening. Following their pleasant conversation, President Castro came all the way to the elevator to see him and the other BWA officials off. When they arrived at the elevator, President Castro offered a kindness Billy had not expected.

"Please use the bathroom before you leave."

"That's okay," replied Billy.

"You're going straight to the conference. How will you be able to hold it?" Castro asked.

"I cannot hold up your national attendants for my personal business!" Billy continued. Already, they had become friends. Finally, he agreed to go to the bathroom before the rally. Yet, Billy's heart was deeply content. The meeting had lasted two hours twenty minutes. Later, he found out that this meeting had been longer than when Castro had met with Pope John Paul II.

President Castro, in return for the gift of the Bible, had sent the minister and vice-minister of religion, along with six government-run TV cameras, to the conference site. The following day, without any prior arrangements, the evangelistic conference details were aired for one whole hour, during a government-run prime-time TV broadcast. The "latter rain" of the gospel was pouring down throughout all of Cuba.

Billy prayed a thankful prayer inside the plane, as he was departing Havana. As he sat pondering the events of the past few days, he began to reminisce. Standing in front of him, in Billy's mind, was a small young boy, wearing a huge khaki-colored US Army uniform, carelessly stitched, and altered here and there, to fit him.

It was the houseboy, back in Korea.

HAVE FAITH IN GOD

His father was a poor peasant farmer in a rural village. His mother had given birth to eight children. However, four died at birth or shortly after, and she was full of sadness as she raised the remaining four children. Then Jang Hwan (Billy) Kim[1] was born. Later the Kims had a tenth child, who died at age three after she drank a cleanser she thought was water, which had been left on the outside wooden step. His mother always seemed to feel sad that five of her children did not survive. He was now the youngest of the remaining five.

After World War II and the country's liberation from Japan, his family moved to Suwon, twenty miles south of Korea's present capital, Seoul. There Billy began attending a six-year agriculture and forestry school. His course of study would be three years in the middle school plus three years in high school. Attending the school had seemed a nearly impossible dream to this son of an impoverished peasant farmer. Prospective students had to pass a stringent entry test to enter what was essentially a professional school about agriculture. Then there would be the cost of six years of education. But his mother and he knew admittance to a vocational school almost assured later entry into the workforce.

Billy passed the test, but his funds were limited. The farm villages had no financial programs to assist with an education. Although there was no tuition, monthly supplemental fees would add up. He could only help his older brother load cow-carts with rice and deliver the food all around the rural area. He had to get up at dawn to make gruel of beans and straw for the cattle, only to receive a little pocket change. Billy's oldest brother and his mother tried to help him pay these monthly fees.

A DREAM OF BECOMING A STATIONMASTER

Three years passed as he struggled to pay for his education; he made the fees payments either just on the due date or late. Continuing into high school seemed unthinkable. However, if he was unable to go to high school, it would be impossible for him to accomplish his elementary school dream of becoming a politician, or his middle school dream of becoming the minister of agriculture and forestry. Whatever it took, he was determined to continue his education.

Then he found a way to continue into high school. He could enter the government-funded Railroad High School located in Yongsan, Seoul. He had heard that not only was it tuition and fee free, but they even gave students an allowance! It would move him away from agriculture, but graduating from the Railroad High School and becoming his hometown Suwon stationmaster sounded pretty good!

Billy got choked up at the mere possibility of continuing his education.

On June 25, 1950, North Korea invaded South Korea with 135,000 troops. Yet Jang Hwan's (Billy's) family was totally unaware that the Korean War had just begun. Like on any other day of the previous years, his family was busy transplanting rice seedlings. On the following day, he left for Seoul to take the Railroad High School entrance exam. He kept hearing booming sounds, yet never realized that they were indications of war.

He was planning to stay at his uncle's house, so his mother packed him a five-gallon bag of barley to give for the cost of his lodging. He grabbed the bag and followed the men from his village who were working at the Seoul railroad, as they got on the train headed toward Seoul.

A DREAM ENDED

After he arrived at his uncle's house, he dropped his bag of books and barely and got on the tram to the Railroad High School. When he arrived, he saw that the school's iron gates were shut tight with a public notice posted: "Entrance Exam Indefinitely Postponed." Then, he heard loud, continuous explosions from somewhere close by. Though still very young, he knew that something unusual was happening. He stopped a man who was urgently rushing past the school.

"Sir, what's all the commotion? Is something wrong?"

"The People's Republic Army has already invaded the hills of Miahri," the man said.

Jang Hwan decided against going back to his uncle's house to retrieve his books and barley, and returned quickly to the Seoul Railway Station. The trains had stopped operating.

Boom! Boom! Ba . . . Booooom . . . Boom! Just over one hundred feet in front of him, several bombs exploded in succession. A mother ran away, abandoning her own child. The People's Republic Army from the north, under Soviet influence, had extended its invasion into the south. Airplanes indiscriminately continued bombing for several minutes. Although his heart should be trembling in fear, everything was so unfamiliar to him that it was strangely fascinating.

Jang Hwan stayed alive by hiding under the vehicle wheels. After the planes had passed by, he kept on walking along the railroad. He was fortunate to be able to hitch a ride on a loaded train and safely arrive at his home in Suwon.

Though he had arrived back home, his family did not evacuate but chose to remain in Suwon to face the Korean War that now overtook their area. Soon, the People's Republic Army seized Suwon. Their leader called out people from place to place and formed them into groups, with names that no one had heard before.

The invading army placed the cow-cart of Jang Hwan's older brother under requisition. However, through the ingenuity of their mother, not even one member of the family was forced to join the militia or become involved with the militia army, and they were all unharmed.

Three months would pass. By September 28, 1950, the news had spread . . . Seoul had been recovered! Their town was now free of the invaders, although the Korean War would continue until July 27, 1953, taking the lives of more than five million soldiers and civilians.[2]

To a young sixteen-year-old, war was not a scary thing. After the recovery of Seoul, Suwon was no longer an immediate battleground and it was hard to feel the war, but there were still evidences of the war.

Most schools were so devastated and ruined by the bombings that they could not accept any students. Jang Hwan and other young boys of his age could no longer go to school and spent their days doing household chores to help their parents. Jang Hwan and his friends were responsible to chop wood to use as household fuel. The main logging area was four kilometers away from home. After breakfast, he met eight of his friends to collect firewood.

A VISIT TO THE US ARMY 21ST REGIMENT

At three or four in the afternoon, they finished their logging, and they always stopped by the Suwon prison on their way home, because the United States Army 24th Division, 21st Regiment, was stationed there. The boys stopped not to talk with their American defenders but in hopes of the chocolates and chewing gum that the soldiers would sometimes give them. As they prowled inside the fence, if they were fortunate, the schoolboys would meet a sympathetic US Army soldier.

Then one day . . . young Jang Hwan received something much more important than chocolate or gum! As on any other day, he and his friends were snooping for some sweets. One soldier saw them and pointed directly at Jang Hwan, beckoning him to come inside the barracks.

Jang Hwan was not sure what would happen but stepped forward. Years later, after he had faith in Christ, Billy would realize that the soldier's pointing finger was that of God—God had been drawing Jang Hwan to Himself. In this moment, a verse from God's Word proved to be true in Jang Hwan's life. Isaiah 43:1 says, "I have summoned you by name; you are mine" (NIV). It was as though the Lord's hand had led young Jang Hwan to come inside the barracks.

The US Army soldier pointed toward the stove heater and spoke a few words in English. Not understanding a single word, Jang Hwan easily understood by his gesturing that he was to build a fire in the stove. Jang Hwan ran out, took straw from the field, started a fire in the stove, and fanned the flames to keep the fire going.

As he gazed into the flames, the boy noticed that the barracks were in shambles. So he washed the dishes; then he shook and dusted off the blanket and hung it in the bright sun. Next he shined the dirty army boots and reorganized everything into a neat and tidy condition. This was easy work compared to his household chores, working in the fields since childhood, logging and collecting wood, and having to walk back and forth three hours every day.

When he was almost done cleaning, the soldier came back inside his barracks. His eyes opened wide with surprise. He raised his hands and gave Jang Hwan a big "thumbs-up," his face showing his satisfaction.

The boy knew he was "saying" something else: "Come back again tomorrow!"

MEET THE HOUSEBOY

This was the beginning of Jang Hwan's days as a "houseboy." Houseboys had no set wages. They were given instead cigarettes, chocolates, chewing gum, and stick candies—all part of the rations that soldiers received every five days. What the GIs didn't need became currency for the houseboys.

Among the American goods, the cigarette was the most welcome payment. In those days, American cigarettes included Kool, Lucky Strike, Camel, Chesterfield, and Philip Morris. The most expensive of these was Kool. Just one pack would sell for 4,000 won in the so-called Yankees' black market. In wartime Korea, this payment was equivalent to five huge loads of wood. The entire family was able live better because of Jang Hwan's part-time job.

But only a week later, there was a shift in the state of the war. The Chinese Red Army was invading Korea from the north! The US Army began relocating to the south, until finally only a few soldiers remained.

The soldiers suggested that Jang Hwan leave with them. He wanted to follow them, but his mother adamantly tried to dissuade him.

"Jang Hwan, even if we are to die, let's face death together here."

"DIE IF YOU WILL. GO!"

Giving up on going, he headed back to the Suwon prison site in hopes of scavenging leftover goods from the US Army soldiers. As the soldiers saw Jang Hwan, they urged him again to join them in going. Seeing them finalize their preparations to depart made his heart burn with desire to follow them.

He asked them to wait while he ran back to his home. He begged his mother in tears.

"Die if you will. GO!"

Without a moment's hesitation after his mother's permission, he ran, not turning back, straight to the US Army base and jumped onto the army truck. All he had heard from his mother's statement was one word, "GO!"

That was Christmas Day 1950.

He was assigned to one of the four barracks. Now he was in charge of helping some twenty American soldiers. His living style had not changed from his days in Suwon as a houseboy, except now, he didn't have a home to go back to in the evenings.

"GOOD MORNING, BILLY!"

The supply goods delivery that came every five days was pure bliss. Besides the cigarettes, chocolates, and chewing gum, the soldiers enjoyed canned food, coffee, socks, parkas, underwear, etc. Everything they needed was there, and as time passed, Billy's payment in cash-equivalent goods was piling up nicely in his secret storage container.

Life at the barracks was extremely busy. Yet Jang Hwan, who was now sixteen, trembled like a small bird in his loneliness. The region had many orchards filled with apple trees. Every time he missed his mother and family, he would sit under an apple tree and play his harmonica.

"Good morning, Billy!" It was Sergeant Carl Powers. He was from the neighboring barracks and in charge of personnel there. Jang Hwan knew him to be very kind and that he didn't drink or smoke. The American soldiers thought Jang Hwan's name was too difficult to pronounce, so they gave him an American name. Now he was simply "Billy."

He greeted Carl merely by glancing with his eyes as he continued playing his harmonica. But then Carl held Billy's small shoulders as he said, "Would you like to go to America?"

Suddenly, Billy took his mouth away from his harmonica, looked at Carl's face, and without hesitation answered, "Yes!"

Whenever idle from barracks work, he had indulged himself in reading the American Sears Roebuck catalogue. Inside were pictures and descriptions of things he had never seen before. He wanted to go to America so that he could see them in person.

Later, he realized that Carl had paid close attention to him from the first day he had arrived. Billy had jumped off the truck and warmly greeted other American soldiers as if they had been longtime friends. This left a strong impression on Carl. After that day and the very special invitation to visit America with him, Billy made a point of spending more time with Carl.

Pale, pinkish-white apple blossoms bloomed and then withered at the army camp. In their place were quite greenish apples, each about the size of a plum. About this time, the winds of the war shifted again.

YEARNING TO BE HOME

The Korean Army was gaining ground northward. The US Army naturally retraced their steps north as well. Carl was relocated to the front line and for a while, Billy was unable to see him. Even so, he was nearer to his hometown in Suwon. He began to yearn to see his mother and family, so much that soon it seemed too much to bear.

Eventually he acted on his desires. After five months, Billy had filled his storage container with GI rations, including candies, treats, and especially cigarettes. He rushed to visit the nearest carpenter and had him make two wooden crates. One he filled with the cigarettes. The other he piled up with canned goods, chocolates, and other things that could be sold at the Yankees' black market. He asked a jeep-driving soldier he had come to know if he could hitch a ride. The driver was glad to give Billy a lift home.

Imagine the scene of a "houseboy" who had left with the US Army soldiers returning to his hometown on an American Army jeep, loaded with two wooden crates full of American goods, while still in the middle of a war. Not even a parade held for an Olympic gold medalist would have caused more of a stir among the hometown folks than he did.

His heart was pounding as he rode home . . .

"Mom!" Among the surprised town people, he saw his mother. He jumped off the jeep before it could stop and ran to her. He was in his mother's arms . . . !

Ah! . . . My mother's scent. His senses revived. It now seemed much longer than six months away from home.

"Jang Hwan! You came back alive!" His mother's roughened hands continually patted her youngest son's back. Her feelings of blame and sorrow, relief and joy, made his heart pound. Between the mother and son, many tears fell.

He sold the two wooden crates of American goods at the Yankees' black market. It provided greater profit than he had hoped. He gave the money to his older brother who had lost his delivery business when the People's Republic had requisitioned his cow-cart.

"Brother, you're going to take care of my tuition now."

AN AMERICAN HIGH SCHOOL EDUCATION?

Billy was determined to go back to school and give up the life of a houseboy. He ran back to the Suwon agriculture and forestry school, only to see a large sign posted on the main door: "No Classes Until Further Notice." Bomb-ruined schools were in no condition to accept students anytime soon. God redirected him back to the US military headquarters.

After returning to the headquarters, Billy watched as the mobile base moved farther north toward the North Han River. The soldiers began ongoing military maneuvers to keep the enemy off guard, while the houseboys stayed at the division headquarters and waited for the GIs' return.

Each time the base relocated, Carl would try to visit Billy.

Each time Carl could visit, Billy would become more determined to go to America. And each time Carl asked if he still wanted to go to America, he would answer with a determined heart, "Yes!"

Still, nothing seemed to happen. Billy began to question in his mind whether Carl would really take him to America and wondered if perhaps Carl was only teasing him. Repeated disappointments drained his hopes, making him feel helpless. His dreams and desires to go to America, built up through Sears Roebuck catalogues, began to wane.

Then one day, Carl visited Billy. "Billy, sign here!" He held out a document in English. It was an admissions application to an American high school called Bob Jones Academy. All the blank areas had been filled in by Carl. Billy was not a Christian, but something told him that he could trust Carl to keep his promises of sending him to school if he went with him to America. Billy would not understand anything about Christianity even if Carl had attempted to explain Bob Jones Academy's Christian faith principles. But the teenage houseboy dreamed of receiving a better education in America, especially since all Korean schools were closed throughout the war. The boy signed the paper. Sergeant Carl grabbed the papers in one hand and patted Billy's shoulder with the other, and then he walked away.

Of course, Billy had no idea what God had planned for him. Moreover, Carl had no opportunities to visit him for several months. Occasionally, Billy thought about words like *Sears Roebuck, America, Sergeant Carl Powers*, and *admissions application* . . . but now, he didn't expect much from it.

FEAR INSTEAD OF JOY

On May 25, 1951, a letter arrived from Bob Jones Academy in Greenville, South Carolina. The letter of acceptance welcomed Jang Hwan—"Billy"—to the academy. The next day the army ordered Carl to return to the United States. Together the two events should have brought rejoicing to the houseboy. But after Carl presented the letter, Billy felt a sudden fear instead of joy.

"I don't think my mom will let me go," he told Sergeant Carl. Yet equally troubling to Billy was his limited English. All the English he knew were a few simple words and some swear words used during a couple of months' stay in the barracks with the soldiers. The language limits plus the fact that he didn't know anyone in America had suddenly frightened him.

Carl just stood up and left the barracks, without saying a word. The look of his weary, drooping shoulders seemed very sad. Long, conflicting hours passed by sluggishly. After a few days, Carl returned.

"Billy, you will grow taller. Don't worry about English, you will be good at it in a short time, and if your mother disapproves, I'll get her permission." Carl was more serious than he had ever been previously.

Later, Billy would learn that Carl had postponed his opportunity to be stationed back in the States just to be able to help him with the school's admission process.

Still, Billy squatted down, lowered his head, and drew meaningless symbols on the ground.

"Billy, don't miss this chance." Carl held Billy's shoulders with his hands. Then Billy noticed in Carl's eyes the kind, heartfelt tears. But Billy still felt he could not go to America.

Several hours later, Carl reappeared, this time with someone else. "Billy, get in the jeep!" Carl's eyes were glaring with grave determination. The person in the vehicle seemed like an interpreter.

Billy got on, thinking that his mother would never allow it. He simply got on the jeep as his last gesture of friendship and appreciation toward Carl for his efforts. Then Carl drove them to Billy's home in Suwon.

FIND THE
SOURCE OF FAITH

Billy's mother wore a smile upon seeing her son in the Jeep. But who was this soldier? Her face quickly turned cold and stern as she met Sergeant Powers for the first time.

Seeing his mother's expression reminded Billy of his pet dog during his childhood, a gold-colored female mutt. One day, the mutt got pregnant and within a couple of months became a mom to seven pups. Those golden pups were so charming and cute. Billy wanted to take the cutest pup and show it to his friends. Billy was shocked when he tried to reach into the mutt's bed to grab a puppy. Her eyes flashed and her fierce canine teeth gnashed at him. She was not the gentle, friendly mutt that he had known; she had the fierce, protective eyes of a mother glaring at the intruder of her pups.

His mom now had the eyes of those puppies' mother, Billy thought, as she stared coldly at Carl. She had heard numerous, unsavory rumors after the Korean War started about American soldiers and Korean women. Now, as she faced Carl, those rumors of selfish, even arrogant GIs flooded her mind. She probably visualized the gruesome image of her loving, youngest son dying and being thrown away in the back alleys of America, after being exploited by a callous American soldier for labor in a foreign country.

To a widowed mother, being told of this "invitation" to give up her bright, amiable, youngest boy must have seemed more than she could bear. Carl, who had seemed truly determined before visiting Billy's home, could not say a word to her piercing looks and unspoken fears. The silence seemed to last for a long time.

"How many years must he stay in America?" It was his mother who first broke the silence.

"Including high school and college, about seven years, I believe." Then, his mother asked a few more questions about the process of getting to America, and what kind of life he would be living in America. Throughout the conversation, Billy sat in the corner, observing both parties go back and forth with questions and answers, the translator in the middle of it all. The teen sat with an expressionless face, as if he were an uncertain judge in a court of law.

Again, silence from his mother.

A TEARFUL DECISION

Billy looked closely at his mother. Her teary eyes were filled with worries and fears for her son. And she began to cry—as if she had come to a decision. Yet she recognized an unusual opportunity for her son in America. Life in Korea had been terribly difficult and would continue to be so for some time even if South Korea were freed from the North. If her son went to the United States with Sergeant Powers, he could receive further education and also mature as a healthy adult.

She concluded she had little other choice for his welfare in a war-torn country. She would put her trust in Sergeant Carl.

A moment later she spoke with a gentle, quiet, and yet shaky voice.

"You can take Jang Hwan with you."

God had purposed to send Billy to America. God had moved on his mother's heart.

Once more Mrs. Kim had agreed to let her son leave home to be with the American military—but this time to leave not only his home but his country. With her consent, Carl began to secure the documents necessary for Billy to study abroad.

A LONG AND WINDING ROAD

It would not be easy to send an unaccompanied minor to the United States during wartime. Moreover, Carl was still on active war duty. The approval by the Korean and American governments would be almost as tough as receiving Mrs. Kim's permission.

The process for approving Billy's studies abroad became a long and winding road. During the war, the United States embassy and the Korean government had relocated to the southernmost coastal city, called Pusan (known as Busan since 2000). Carl dedicated his efforts to going back and forth from the US embassy to the Korean government office, and then going from his northern frontline army duty station down to Pusan in the south to meticulously arrange Billy's departure. Sergeant Powers worked diligently to receive the Korean government's permission to let a minor depart his country in the middle of a continuing war.

Much later Billy found out that Carl had postponed going back to his country and being stationed in the United States *five times* just to help the teen. It was truly unbelievable to the onetime houseboy—a kindness beyond what a person does even for immediate family members.

Carl was not a Christian at that time. Yet God moved Carl's heart and worked through him for Billy. It was truly an example of how God does things beyond our knowledge and understanding. Although not a Christian, the sergeant chose to look after Billy's welfare by sending him to a Christian school in America.

In September 1951 all the papers were completed, enabling Billy to finally go to the United States.

Even though all the documents had been processed and cleared, the visa had not yet arrived. Once again, Carl ran here and there, writing and submitting petitions to the Korean government representatives, and elsewhere. Finally, the visa was issued.

Until this moment, Billy had done absolutely nothing. It had all been possible through Carl's tireless efforts.

The ship that was to take Billy to America was a US supplies transport vessel. These vessels, after unloading the American supplies in Korea, would take on passengers returning to the United States. The cost for one passenger was a hefty $408. This was an enormous amount for anyone in 1951 dollars. Carl handed Billy a one-way ticket to America.

I am really going to America! he thought to himself with a pounding heart. He returned to Suwon to say his last goodbye to his mother.

After he gave a deep bow toward the ground, his mother handed him a small pouch of woven hemp cloth, with handmade stitches holding the strings that were tied on top.

"Whenever you miss home, boil it and drink it." It was a handful of homeland soil from his vegetable garden.

Billy packed the pouch of soil inside his duffel bag and went all the way south, to Pusan. There he boarded the ship to America. But Carl was not on the ship to America on November 12, 1951. He couldn't go with Billy because his extension to serve in Korea would not end until the beginning of December.

A ROCKY TRIP TO THE NEW WORLD

The supply ship left port, and for two days Billy endured, almost unconscious with motion sickness. Three or four more days passed, and he slowly adjusted, the nausea subsiding. Then the haunting thoughts of fear returned. What awaited in America, especially without the sergeant? *Why did Carl extend his stay in Korea, postponing his return to the United States, and why did he spend so much money just to take me to America?*

He could not understand the soldier's help. With only the relationship of a houseboy to a sergeant in the US Army, it made no sense that Sergeant Powers would sacrifice so much for him. As Billy walked on the deck of the ship, these questions repeatedly tortured his mind.

Four other Korean students were on board, all in their midtwenties. They had already graduated from the university and were on their way to further study abroad. By their clothing, it was evident that they were from wealthy Korean families. No one's situation was like his.

I've got it. He is taking me to use as a slave. As he thought of it, he recalled Carl mentioning one day that his parents were farmers in the States. He could not sleep as he worried about his future.

Not all weather can be perfect during a forty-day sail across the open seas. On one occasion, the ship headed into a massive storm. Huge waves the size of houses poured on the deck. The waves tossed the big ship, and once more his stomach churned with motion sickness. Sudden fear overcame him—*the ship will break in half!* He really thought he would not see tomorrow.

Suddenly, his mother's words came to his mind. "Die if you will. GO!" Before, only the word "GO!" kept ringing in his ears, but now only the words "Die if you will" kept circling in his mind. And then an image of his mother getting up early in the morning with a bowl of water, to offer prayers to the sky came to his mind.

Without realizing it, he was praying. "God above, please save me this once, and I'll live to help many people."

Billy did not know God, yet God heard his prayers. God must have laughed, "Billy, you *are* going to meet Me."

After some time, the ocean became calm once more. Rough waves make a skilled boatman, and tough times make a boy into a young man. Gone with the rough waves were the doubts and anxieties about Carl, his benefactor. With his life restored, there was nothing to fear, he concluded.

"I AM REALLY IN AMERICA!"

On December 23, exactly six weeks after he boarded the ship, he arrived in San Francisco. Dazzling Christmas lights seemed to greet Billy from almost every building. Today in Korea, the streets are filled with glittering lights during Christmastime, but in those days most of Korea was lit only by kerosene lamps. His first impression of America was of a country of brilliant lights.

As he got off the ship and made his first step on American ground, Billy fully realized, "Yes, I am really in America!"

Walking down on the exit ramp, he had touched his name tag on his jacket, to make certain it was showing. His mother had stitched his name in large print on the left side of his baggy army jacket, so that the people who were to pick him up could recognize him.

Lieutenant Heim, whom he had met in Korea, was there to pick him up. A friend standing with the lieutenant first recognized "Billy" as they waved at him from behind the exit ramp. Meanwhile Carl had prearranged for his corporal to make certain of all landing documents, and to meticulously make sure that everything was prepared for Billy's arrival. Billy passed through US immigration and customs without any problems and headed out to the lieutenant's house.

San Francisco near Christmastime was sheer magnificence. The shopping center show windows were wonderfully decorated. The streets were filled with cars, and people bustled about, loaded with gift packages. Amazing curves and lines showed the grandness of the Golden Gate Bridge.

To a country boy from Korea, not only San Francisco but also the majestic grandeur of America was surely the image of a new world.

SHOPPING IN AMERICA

Those welcoming Billy to America must have felt bad seeing him in the rough, now-shrunken army clothes the sergeant had given him. On the following day, the lieutenant's mother took him to buy some new clothes. He entered the shopping mall. There before him were all the things he had seen in the catalogue of Sears Roebuck, but it was unbelievably real, displayed on shelves, right in front of young Billy's face.

Like a country bumpkin, he gazed in amazement at the displays. They went to the clothing section; there he tried on a shirt, necktie, and jacket they had picked out for him. He stood in front of the mirror, dazed and surprised to see an unaccustomed reflection of himself.

The next few days were surreal, immersed in the excitement of the new world. For the next couple of days, Billy's thoughts filled with rose-colored dreams of his future, aided by the kind and generous help of the lieutenant's family.

Nevertheless, as the last days of the year passed, he heard no news from Carl. The anxiety that he thought he had left under the ship's deck slowly started to creep back. To make matters worse, the date to start school, according to the admissions letter of acceptance, was January 23.

Will I really be able to go to school? A shadow of doubt always lurks outside a nomad's tent. While seemingly keeping his composure, he paced daily in the vicinity of the telephone.

A CALL FROM CARL

Finally, in the middle of January, a call came from Carl.

Though he was sad in leaving Lieutenant Heim's family, Billy ultimately needed to go to Carl's home in Virginia. However, the way to get to Virginia was not simple. He would have to change buses several times across the vast land to reach Ohio. Then, he would meet Carl's older brother, who lived there, and drive nine more hours to get to Carl's home.

When Billy arrived at the bus terminal with Lieutenant Heim's family, the staff person said that they would not be able to issue him a ticket. Not only was he too young to ride on his own, but he couldn't speak English. They explained that they didn't want to deal with a lawsuit, in case he got lost on the way.

The only way was to take a direct flight without any layovers. The problem with this was the cost. The airline ticket was $156 and all he had was $130. Carl had given him $100 and $30 was cash he had saved from selling G.I. rations as a houseboy.

The lieutenant thought over the possibilities. Then he came up with an idea.

The airline allowed children under twelve to board with a 50 percent discount. Billy's height was like an eleven-year-old American boy, so the lieutenant thought he could easily pass for under twelve.

In addition, Billy's passport was only a one sheet document in Korean and Chinese characters, indicating his birthday as being July 25, according to the Korean Dangun Era based 4,267th year. There was no way the staff of the airline could know his actual age.

The quick thinking of the lieutenant worked perfectly. He was able to purchase the TWA plane ticket for half the regular price to Ohio. The flight took a rather long four hours thirty minutes. The distance was longer than Billy thought.

He wanted to meet Carl right away, but he still had to wait until the weekend, when Carl's older brother was off work and could drive Billy the nine hours from Ohio to Carl's place in Dante, Virginia.

MORE DOUBTS AND FEARS

When Billy stepped out of the car, he was surprised and disappointed. Carl's farmhouse was in secluded woods much deeper than Billy's farmhouse. The glitter of San Francisco was just a mirage to lure him to this dark place, he thought, and he fell into despair.

Hidden behind the gentle smile of Carl was the crafty scheme of a farm owner, Billy figured. Looking around the front yard, he became convinced that they had brought him here as a slave. He was in despair—there was no school around anywhere. The admissions letter of acceptance might have been fake.

That night, as he sat around the dinner table with Carl and his family, he smiled as if nothing was wrong, but his doubts and fears grew bigger and bigger, as the family's laughter and kindness increased.

Ninety-nine percent of our worries do not become a reality. And so on February 3, 1952, just weeks after arriving at Carl's home, Billy was able to start school. Carl's promise was real, and Billy's worries were not. It was impossible to visually see Bob Jones Academy in South Carolina from deep in the woods of Virginia. But it was there, waiting for the young student from Suwon, Korea.

He proudly entered Bob Jones Academy in Greenville, South Carolina. He started classes the next day as a ninth grader. It was already the second week of the spring quarter.

Carl had completed all the documents required for final admission and had paid for his tuition, including dormitory fees. As Carl turned and left the campus, Billy desperately tried to voice his thanks audibly.

"Carl! I'm sorry . . . and . . . I thank you . . . truly!" he shouted into the silence.

WAITING TO MEET GOD

Bob Jones Academy is a private school founded by evangelist Bob Jones Sr. in 1927, originally for students in grades seven through twelve. Today it includes all grades, from kindergarten through grade twelve. The school was founded on and stands by its fundamentalist Christian beliefs, and all students are required to live by its historically strict principles, consistent with a conservative Christian faith. Its sister institution, Bob Jones College (now Bob Jones University), was also founded in 1927 near Panama City, Florida, with the same Christian standards of faith.

Again, Carl had not yet become a Christian, yet he chose this strict Christian private school for Billy to attend. Why did Carl choose Bob Jones Academy (BJA) for Billy? Public school was free, but BJA had its tuition charges, as most private schools do. If it wasn't for the cost, what could have been his motive? Carl had heard of the solid academic reputation of the academy and wanted the best for his loyal houseboy. BJA, which has relocated to Greenville, South Carolina, was in his "neck of the woods," just 190 miles from Carl's home in Dante, Virginia.

Sometime after that, the One who had called him to Bob Jones began to move Billy's heart. It was not at the daily chapel service, where he couldn't understand the content of worship in English. And though students from several rooms in the residence hall met for dorm worship every night, to Billy it seemed like an unfamiliar ritual of a foreign religion.

God certainly did not woo Billy through the teachers' lectures during the classes, whose words in English were like the "static noises" of an inaudible radio frequency. To add to these troubles, the food in the cafeteria was totally not what he was used to.

Surrounded by the four walls of the dormitory, Billy felt caged inside a dark, narrow, and tall-ceilinged box, all alone. He cried in intense loneliness.

"Mom, Mom, Mother!" He missed his mother. He yearned desperately for his mother's homemade bean stew. He felt as if someone had cut open his heart and was rubbing it with a tough pot scrubber. Billy was extremely homesick.

One day, Pastor Dong Myung Kim and his wife, Esther Ahn Kim, visited him. Esther Ahn Kim (Yi Sook Ahn) had been imprisoned and persecuted for her Christian faith during World War II; later she would write the moving story of God's faithfulness in a bestselling book, *If I Perish*.[1] Dong Myung and Esther were currently students at Bob Jones Graduate School. They had heard of a Korean student who had enrolled and had come to visit. They invited him to their house and kindly provided him with a Korean meal.

ALL ALONE

As he left their house, they gave him a Bible as a gift. Yet, he did not read it. For the first time in a long while, he had met with Koreans, chatted in Korean, and eaten Korean food. Even so, neither his loneliness, nor his longing for home, subsided. And he did not look for God . . . not yet.

And his aloneness became worse and even deeper.

The mere falling of an autumn leaf would bring tears to his eyes. A gaze into the moonlit night would intensify the aches in his heart. He knew that the moon was the same as the moon from the night sky of his homeland, and he could almost see his mother's face on the glowing moon. Many nights he sat by his window, gazing at the moon, unaware of his falling tears. He remembered a line from a song back home: "Gazing at the glowing moon, not even the loneliness passes soon."

He cried as he looked at the moon. He cried and cried with thoughts of his mother.

MEETING GOD

Billy's ability to understand and speak the English language grew as his roommate, Jerry Thompson, helped him with impromptu lessons throughout the first semester. Then later in the semester another Jerry on the dorm floor had just hung his laundry and stepped outside his room, where he noticed the international student in the hallway. Jerry Major, himself a college freshman at Bob Jones University, introduced himself. Billy told him about his soldier friend who brought him to America and the academy. Billy admitted he was feeling alone at school, and Jerry invited him into his room to continue their conversation.

There Jerry Major would open his Bible to John 3:16 and asked Billy to read it.

"For God . . . so loved the world . . . that he gave . . . his one and only Son . . . that whoever . . . believes in him . . . shall not perish . . . but have . . . eternal life" (NIV).

Suddenly, Billy felt a rush of emotion he had never felt during chapel or dorm worship. Furthermore, he was captured by a vague expectation that perhaps the "One called Jesus" could quench his urgent thirst for home and mother.

He asked, holding back his tears, "Jerry, I cry every day. I can't study anymore. I think I'll go insane this way. Do you think that this 'Jesus' can help me?"

"Billy, Jesus will most definitely help you. Believe in Jesus, and you will not cry in such despair anymore." Jerry shared the gospel: God sent His only Son to this world to save sinners and chose death on the cross in their place. He then rose again from death and ascended into heaven to forgive all our sins. If anyone believes Jesus did this to save them, they will eternally, forever be saved and will be blessed as God's own child.

Then Jerry asked that they pray together. Billy followed Jerry as he knelt down, hands folded.

"God."

"I am a sinner."

"I accept Jesus who died on the cross for my sins into my heart right now."

"Please forgive my sins."

Billy repeated each line of the prayer as Jerry led. "God, I am a sinner. . . . Please forgive my sins." It was the first time in his life for him to openly pray this way.

At first, it seemed awkward, but as he continued, his heart started to melt. The divine One who had called Billy to Bob Jones was now personally touching Billy's despairing, aching heart and his weary soul, at that very moment.

Jerry was wholeheartedly helping him in his prayer. As the prayer finished, Jerry gave him a hug and explained, "Billy, you just accepted Jesus Christ as your Savior."

HELD IN THE SAVIOR'S ARMS

Moments later, he felt immersed in an indescribable sea of peace. "You have been saved. You are born again," Jerry said. And Billy left the room in joy.[2]

Jerry Thompson was in the college infirmary that day, fighting the flu. When he finally returned to his room, Billy immediately told his roommate he had become a Christian. "But I would have known without him telling me," Jerry recalled later. "His character had changed."[3] . . .

All alone, yet Billy was not alone anymore. The "One" who had called Billy to Bob Jones Academy was with him. Unexplainably, the loneliness was gone. There, Billy met God. There, Billy was saved. There, Billy became a child of God. He now knew the truth: "To all who received him, who believed in his [Jesus'] name, he gave the right to become children of God" (John 1:12 NIV). From there, Billy began his calling to spread the gospel.

EARNESTLY
SHARE THE GOSPEL
ON ANY GIVEN DAY

Billy's life had completely changed after meeting the Lord. Most of all, he focused on his studies.

His roommate, Jerry Thompson, helped him a lot. However, catching up with his studies, all in English, had not been easy. After the final tests, though he could not escape failing in some classes, his teachers thought highly of Billy's efforts and promoted him to the next grade with a "D" average. He pushed himself to study harder as he began his sophomore year.

During vacation breaks, Billy went to help Sergeant Carl. He learned that the ex-soldier was studying hard himself, yet as he tried to pay for Billy's tuition and his own college costs, Carl was struggling financially, despite educational aid through the GI Bill. Considering that a bottle of Coca-Cola sold for five cents during those days, Bob Jones Academy's annual tuition of $730 was a significant amount of money.

Carl worked so hard for him, and now Billy wanted to make Carl happy. An opportunity to do this came early in his sophomore year. He decided to enter a national speech contest. Billy stuttered to correctly pronounce even the shortest everyday English words and to enter the American National Speech Contest was almost unimaginable. However, after meeting God, he became confident in everything.

MEETING GOD BRINGS MIRACLES

He stayed up all night preparing a speech script. Then he submitted it to the teacher, expressing his intent to enter the competition. His teacher, after reviewing it, raised her thumb and exclaimed, "Billy, this is great!" It seemed that the teacher was highly impressed that an Asian student actually had the courage to participate in a national speech contest.

The teacher began Billy's intense training for the speech contest that same day. The most difficult task was to master the enunciation difference between the letters R and L. He strenuously practiced with a marble in his mouth.

At last, the day came for the first round of the speech contest to be held in his school. Billy stood in front of many students and teachers on a footstool, because of his height.

"I am a Korean. I speak for democracy."

His words "I am a Korean" rang through the speakers and came back to his ears. His heart was pounding, and there was an amazing tingling around his tongue.

He could sense the crowd's attention. His pounding heart and the tingling of his tongue worked together to move the audience.

The result was first place!

He was emotionally overwhelmed at hearing he had won the competition, but he tried to keep his composure, because his aim was the national speech contest. Billy's strenuous practice continued for the next level, the county speech contest—and he grabbed first place there as well.

Billy was named "Student of the Week" in his school newspaper. He shared his dreams during his interview with the school newspaper.

"I plan to continue my studies in theology after I graduate from high school. Then I will go back to my hometown, Suwon, in Korea. My sole desire is to go back and share the good news of the gospel with them. I certainly believe that I can accomplish my purpose through the help of my Lord God."

It was exciting enough that as a county speech winner he would be able to compete on the state level. However, he still wanted to compete in the national speech contest.

On the day of the state competition, Billy spoke with even more passion. "I am able to go to school now, thanks to the help of an American Army soldier, Carl. I thank the United States for sending such men to my country and giving me an opportunity to know what democracy is. I also humbly thank the almighty God, for giving me such freedom."

To the American people, who suffered the pain of the Korean War as they sent and lost their loved ones there, a youth from that small country in Asia, shouting out the word "democracy," must have touched their hearts.

He won first place at the state contest. As he walked up to the podium to receive the award, he felt slightly faint, as if this was all a dream, an illusion. Miracles were happening in Billy's life. Would the same miracle occur again at the national speech contest? There was no guarantee.

"Everything is in Your hands, Lord God," he prayed wholeheartedly in silence. And then he stood in front of the crowd at the national competition and shouted out with all his heart:

"You people, who are free, listen to what I say. We live here, guaranteed the freedom of speech, freedom to hold gatherings, freedom to express ourselves, and freedom to worship. On the contrary, on the other side of the world, people live with false promises. Only democracy can guarantee a person's rights and an opportunity for a better education for all. This is what most people desire, and it is possibly the best thing."

The loud applause predicted a good outcome. Among the judges some had teary eyes, even as they gave the speaker their warm applause.

Billy won the first prize, named the Eisenhower Award after President Dwight Eisenhower.

REPAYING CARL IN A SMALL WAY

At the next chapel, Mr. Clough, the academy principal, told students, "When this small young man entered my office for the first time, he couldn't even speak one word in English." This was a miracle possible only by the power of God.

Billy had received a trophy and a television as prizes. During those days in America, a television was a precious possession. In a rural farm area, perhaps only one television was available for the entire town. When he gave it as a gift to Carl's family, together they shed tears of joy.

He felt he had at last repaid Carl, even if only in a small way. It was a joyful time.

A MIRACLE OF LOVE

After the speech contest, Billy suddenly became famous, and this began his active school life. He became involved in a literature club, called Mohegan, and as a team leader of sports activities. He joined a choir and served as a faithful counselor to his classmates. He was also in charge of editing the sports section of *Triangle*, the academy's magazine.

Among his classmates, he was known as an all-around sportsman, an honor student, and a role model, with not even a point deduction on the infamously strict dormitory rules of the school. He was popular and well-liked by female classmates too. He had many opportunities to court female friends.

However, Billy never dated. It was because he could not accept the fondness in their eyes. Billy was still suffering from a deeply embedded inferiority complex. He did not want a girl's sympathetic compassion.

Bob Jones was known for its historical traditions. One of them was for boys to write a letter of invitation to girls to be their partners at several social events at the school. Those who could not find a proper partner would have to go with their classmates, boys with boys, and girls with girls. Billy, as usual, would go with his male friends, not even bothering to write any letters.

But one day, a girl appeared right before his eyes . . . the girl he wanted to go to the music concert with.

"Hi!" She smiled as she walked toward Billy's table.

It was Trudy, a sophomore girl who worked part-time as a student waitress at the school cafeteria. At Bob Jones, most students lived in dorms and ate at the school, and therefore, knew each other at least by name.

On that particular day, Trudy was in charge of serving at Billy's table. The smile of this neat and properly dressed girl caused his heart to start pounding. More than anything, he really liked the fact that she was not so tall. He really wanted to ask her on a date.

Nevertheless, Trudy was well known and popular among the boys, who nicknamed her "Sparkle." She already had many close male friends, one of whom was Bob Jones III (the son of the university president), who later became the president of Bob Jones University.

There is no way that she would accept a date from a foreigner like me . . . , he thought. Love can make one feel belittled and wretched. The more he faced the radiance of her beauty, the more he lacked the courage to ask her. However, nothing could stop his thoughts from moving toward her.

Billy quietly approached the English teacher, who was the teacher on duty that day. *She's the very person to talk to,* thought Billy. He was very thankful for her instruction in English over the past two years.

"Do you think Trudy would accept a date with me?" he whispered.

"Try it!" She smiled with interest. She was also Trudy's English teacher and knew her well. She gladly promised to help Billy.

He decided to write Trudy a letter. From that day on, Billy and the English teacher began to collaborate to win Trudy's heart. The title of this collaboration was "Trudy, My Love!" Their strategy involved a three-step process:

1. Billy first writes the outline of a letter in rough draft.
2. The English teacher refines it with more eloquent words and fine-tunes the paragraph structure.
3. Billy rewrites it in his own handwriting.

Trudy later confessed, after finding out the entire picture of what took place, "I fell into the trap of Billy's inquisitive fondness, and the captivating words of my English teacher."

The tactics succeeded. Trudy accepted Billy's invitation to the music concert. That night, Trudy, in her black velvet top and long dress, was radiantly beautiful. After the music concert, the two continued to build a fond interest in each other through captivating letters.

When they became seniors, they began to officially date. The dates consisted of merely talking to each other from a distance, in a facility called the "date parlor" (according to Bob Jones regulations), or walking on the school grounds, keeping at least fifteen centimeters apart. Even so, Billy was simply happy that Trudy was with him.

Trudy is the best gift God has given me in my life, thought Billy. This was the second miracle, after meeting God. It was a miracle of love.

A MIRACLE OF CALLING

Billy's elementary school dream had been to become a politician. This was during the Japanese forced occupation of Korea. His thought was that as a government patrol officer you wouldn't starve. In his young boy's mind, he needed to become involved in the government so that he could eat white rice and meat-filled soups. Billy, to this day, dislikes barley brown rice, preferring white rice. He feels he has had his lifetime share of barley during his childhood.

During his middle school years at the agriculture and forestry school, he had dreamed of becoming the minister of agriculture and forestry. Later, as he applied for the Railroad High School, he had thought perhaps of becoming a Suwon stationmaster. No matter what he had dreamed in the past, these were not God's plans.

Now as Billy walked on the school grounds during his senior year at Bob Jones Academy, contemplating his college course of study, he heard the command, "You, be My servant!" He decided to become a servant of the Lord, and without hesitation, he decided he would enter the school of theology at Bob Jones University. There he would begin his active involvement in ministries outside of the school.

Even during his high school years, on occasion he would follow his college brothers in Christ to rural churches to share his testimony and offer praises to God. These were evangelistic events, and his role was to assist in various ways. However, as he began his second quarter in college, he began to be invited to these evangelistic events as the main speaker.

The first invitation came from Carl's uncle, who attended Long

Branch Church. It was a small, rural church with only around fifty members. Even though he was asked to share a one-hour "testimony," he was delighted to do so for the glory of God.

First, he spoke of how it had been in Korea. Then, he spoke of the process it took for Carl to bring him to America. A brief explanation of his life at Bob Jones Academy followed.

In the main part, he introduced the God who had called him by name and brought him to America. He did not forget to mention all the miraculous events he had experienced. He spoke of God's plan in his life and included his dreams for serving God in the future.

It was his first solo hour to share his personal testimony, and he made certain it was well organized and clearly stated. After the testimony, someone came up to him.

"Billy, I was greatly moved by your story." It was Mr. Castle, who operated a small store in that town. He invited Billy to his home and served him a wonderful meal, gave him fifty dollars as a scholarship, and encouraged him to study diligently. Afterward, he asked Billy to come to his church to lead an evangelistic event sometime in the coming year. Billy answered that he would gladly do so.

During the next year, Billy kept his promise with Mr. Castle and led an evangelistic event in Dante Baptist Church. After that, other small churches nearby began to invite Billy as well. Even the local Lions Clubs and Rotary Clubs wanted to hear him speak and invited him as a guest speaker. There, too, he shared the good news of the gospel, which resulted in invitations for Billy to come to other churches.

THE YOUNG EVANGELIST

Also, Billy was introduced to the hometown churches of several of his university colleagues, which led to his speaking at many of their evangelistic events. As a theology student, Billy became known around various areas in the United States as an evangelist.

The miracle of his calling had begun. Throughout his college years, evangelistic events were not the only thing he gave his heart to. He earnestly tried to spread the gospel through organizations such as Youth for Christ.

Billy worked during vacation times until the end of his junior year. Even then, he never missed the weekend evangelistic outings. He would leave on Friday afternoons for distant locations and on Saturday mornings for closer places. Often they would go to a rural village known as Extension. They would pass out gospel tracts and invite people to come to church in the evening.

At the church, they would show movies, have a music concert with the Bob Jones musicians, and share the gospel. There were as many as three hundred gathered at times. Many raised their hands high in repentance, and wonderful works of salvation occurred. Many of those students later enrolled at Bob Jones Academy and continued the tradition of going to rural churches on weekends, sharing the good news of the gospel.

In his senior year, he stopped all part-time work during vacations and went to many places, just spreading and sharing the gospel. He was often moved and overwhelmed with joy as he witnessed individual souls coming to Christ.

There, he clearly witnessed the power of the gospel, when so many people were transformed from the death of their souls to salvation. There, in the actual work of missions, moment by moment, he met God. It was there that he came to realize the clear purpose of God for his life. It was a calling. It was a miraculous calling of God for his homeland. He knelt in obedience to his Master.

"I will go back to Korea and live my entire life as an evangelist of the gospel."

MOST JOYFUL MIRACLE

Trudy knew that Billy would return to Korea when he finished graduate school. Still, she had fallen in love with him. Billy loved her, but they had not yet made any marriage plans. It was Trudy's older sister, Peggy, who was determined to make Billy the husband for Trudy. She was the same age as Billy, was well aware of his fame, and had full trust in him.

Peggy was one grade higher than Billy and had graduated from the university the year before. Immediately after her graduation, she was to be married. She invited Billy to recite a word of blessing at her wedding. It was Peggy's brilliant idea to introduce Billy to the members of her family, as Trudy's prospective husband.

The wedding was to take place at Trudy's house in Lakeview, Michigan. If Trudy and Billy were to attend the wedding on Sunday, they had to arrive at the house by Saturday. Billy and Trudy had to drive twenty-four hours straight to arrive in time. The two talked a lot during the car ride. He heard memories of Trudy's childhood and shared his recollections of his own youth.

He got to know about her family stories. Billy told her about his father and mother, his brothers and sisters, and his cousins. They talked over their memories from the first time they had met. They laughed and sometimes shared tears.

He felt guilty and sorry for Trudy, whom he so loved. By now they had agreed to marry, yet he knew that they were going to his economically poor country. She would be with his large family, with lots of work for her to do.

As he drove to her parents' home, the conversation stopped, and there was silence for a while. They could not speak. Time passed unaware. Gently, Trudy took Billy's hand. At that moment, Billy was the happiest person on earth.

When they arrived at Trudy's home, her father was mowing the lawn. Trudy introduced Billy to her father, who greeted him like an old friend he hadn't seen for a long while. Before even entering the house, Billy helped him with the lawn mower as a friendly gesture. When Trudy came outside to the garden with lemonade, they had already become friends.

After finishing the lawn, Trudy's father immediately called his church pastor at Asbury Methodist Church and asked that Billy preach the sermon in the morning. It was an expression of how profoundly confident he was of Billy as a future son-in-law. He also arranged for Billy to give the sermon at the nearby Free Methodist Church on Sunday evening.

Asbury Methodist Church itself had about three hundred members. On that Sunday morning, Billy passionately preached about the God whom he had met. Many in the congregation were teary-eyed and were moved by his message.

On that afternoon, at Peggy's wedding, Billy gave his wholehearted words of blessing. Trudy's father asked many of his friends and well-known associates to come to the Free Methodist Church that evening for worship. It seemed as though Billy's sermon in the morning had strongly touched him. Trudy's father seemingly had already completely accepted him as his future son-in-law.

A CHANCELLOR'S COMMENDATION

After returning from Michigan, Trudy and Billy began officially dating with marriage in mind, and upon her graduation, she told her parents that she wanted to marry him. As expected, her father easily gave permission.

The problem was with her mother. Trudy's mother was not content in her heart with the fact that Billy was an indigent, Asian young man. However, she couldn't unilaterally refuse him in the face of Trudy's determined mindset.

So she decided to visit Bob Jones University and meet with the chancellor before making any final decisions about the marriage. The chancellor told Trudy's mother, "Whether he is American or Asian, Trudy will never be able to find a better husband than Billy."

Trudy and Billy married on August 8, 1958, at 8 p.m. at Greenville Methodist Church in Michigan. For Billy, after meeting God, this was the happiest miracle of his life.

Just prior to this in May, Billy graduated from the school of theology at the Bob Jones University. God had poured grace, like a waterfall, on a boy who was very similar to a war orphan. He was overwhelmed with such an abundant outflowing of grace that all he could do was raise his hands in awe, praising and praying toward the heavens above.

"Oh, Lord, I am the lowest of the humblest of Thy servants." At that very moment, when Billy dedicated himself to be the servant of the Lord, is when God had begun to also raise him up.

MORE MIRACLES

The sweetness of their honeymoon had to end after just one week. He entered the graduate school of Bob Jones University, determined to graduate within a year with a master's degree. He had already completed most of his graduate credit courses during his undergrad years. If he just prepared and completed his master's thesis within a year, it was surely possible. The daily "forced march" of completing his thesis had begun and he was up until 2 a.m. every morning, studying.

Trudy had also rushed to get all her credits in so that she could graduate earlier to accompany Billy to Korea. She graduated from the Bob Jones School of Education sooner than expected and actually started teaching at an elementary school. Therefore, she was as busy as Billy. In addition, she was helping Billy with his thesis and was also working as his secretary.

On February 2, 1959, he was ordained at the Dante Baptist Church in Virginia; that May he received his master's degree in theology. God had completed Pastor Billy Kim's preparation to go to the front line. In prayer, Billy and Trudy prepared to go back to Korea.

The first thing they did was purchase two boat tickets. Then they prayed earnestly for financial support. "God, please help us to find someone who will support us with fifty dollars monthly." They had already purchased the boat tickets, and God's answer also came quickly.

On Wednesday, only a few days before their departure, the Canton Baptist Temple in Ohio had invited Billy as a guest speaker. When Billy declared the words of God, the Holy Spirit moved the heart of the pastor, Harold Henniger. Following the worship service, Pastor Henniger asked them to wait awhile longer.

Led by the Holy Spirit, he held an urgent staff meeting and suggested to them, "Let our church provide the fifty-dollar monthly support for Pastor Billy Kim." At that time, the Canton Baptist Temple sponsored many missionaries, and their usual monthly support amount was $25 per missionary. However, the entire staff, greatly moved by the same Holy Spirit, easily granted the approval of the fifty dollars of monthly support.

It was quite awhile later that Pastor Henniger came back to Billy to let him know what had been decided. "Our church has decided on supporting you, Pastor, with fifty dollars monthly."

Billy fell on his knees. "Lord, thank You. I will boldly go back to my homeland and spread the gospel until my last days." God answered with the exact amount needed, without one dollar difference. For the past fifty years, that church has sent exactly fifty dollars every month (and extra on Christmas).

In addition, God gave him gifts for which he had not asked. Waldo Yeager, whom Billy had always depended on like a father, gave the college graduate much help. Waldo Yeager was the president of Christian Businessmen of America and was the father of Billy's fellow student, Wally Yeager, at Bob Jones Academy. Billy and Wally had become close friends as they worked together during vacations at his father's company.

Upon hearing from Wally of Billy's plan for Korean missions, the older Yeager gathered the socially influential people of Toledo, Ohio, and established an organization called "Christian Service." They appointed Pastor Billy Kim as their missionary sent to Korea from Christian Service, and Trudy Kim as their representative in Korea.

A PICKUP TRUCK FOR KOREA

Adding to all of this, God gave as a bonus a four-wheel-drive Ford pickup truck. Today cars are a common commodity, but in those days, a car was a precious rarity in Korea. Rev. Patrick Doney (also an alumnus of the Bob Jones University School of Theology), who used to officiate as a US Navy chaplain, donated the truck. Doney had become close to Billy during evangelistic functions in the rural churches.

Doney had his own car and never ceased to dedicate his time driving Billy to evangelistic events each week, often totaling over three hundred miles. They had known each other and worked together for over five years. Patrick knew well that on the mission field a car would be an absolute necessity.

He hosted fundraisers to provide Pastor Billy and Trudy with a car. At last, he had successfully raised funds and was able to purchase a four-wheel-drive Ford pickup just prior to their departure. Patrick, Billy, and Trudy were teary-eyed as they watched the truck being loaded onto the ship headed toward Korea.

God was personally making sure that He had supplied everything Billy and Trudy would need. For those who are zealous in spreading the gospel, God for His works' sake will assign His people as companions to the cause.

4

EVANGELIZE, STARTING AT HOME

B illy had two boat tickets to Korea in his hand. However, before he could board the boat, he recalled a debt he needed to pay before leaving America. With Trudy, he visited the San Francisco office of Trans World Airlines (TWA).

"I owe a debt to your company. Eight years ago, I tricked your company. When I was seventeen years old, I used my short height to my advantage. I paid only half the cost of the ticket. I would like to pay the remaining half of that ticket now, before I leave the United States." The woman at the desk shook her head, not understanding, and went to get the assistant manager.

Billy explained in detail what had happened eight years ago. It must have seemed very strange to the TWA manager, as he looked at Billy and Trudy for some time. Then he disappeared inside his office. At last, the manager stepped out.

"Why are you trying to repay the money owed eight years ago?"

"We are a couple leaving as missionaries to Korea in just a few days.

We cannot leave without solving this issue, because of our conscience related to our faith in God. Please help us." Upon their sincere request, the manager called the head office and explained the situation. Then he replied, "Sir, TWA will donate to your mission the remaining half of the ticket. Now, you can forget about it. Thank you for making us delighted today."

The weight on Billy's heart lifted. The Bob Jones schools had taught him the importance of being honest. God had taught him the truth of repentance and forgiveness. Billy knew and believed Jesus' words: "Then you will know the truth, and the truth will set you free" (John 8:32). Only through honest, truthful actions can one truly gain freedom.

THE RETURN HOME

In November 1959, Billy and Trudy got on the boat headed toward Korea. As the boat reached the vast waters of the Pacific Ocean, a seventeen-year-old boy came to Billy's mind. He remembered the boy who had anxiously walked back and forth on the deck of a freighter, only a few US Army clothes packed inside his duffel bag—fearful that he might be sold as a slave.

That very boy had met God, had attended the well-known Bob Jones Academy, and graduated from its university and graduate school with a master of divinity degree. That boy had become a pastor. He also had gained a beautiful American wife.

No one knows why that boy was called to be an evangelist. It was only by the grace of God. It was the divine calling. Still, the unknown future brings fears and uneasiness.

The static Korean words he heard over the radio, barely tuned to the frequency during their crossing of the Pacific, seemed crudely foreign. He had hardly spoken any Korean while in America, and the Korean language had become more awkward than English—not to mention that Trudy was a "complete foreigner," new to the Korean life. "Will we do well?" they wondered.

The confidence he had as they left the States now seemed to be left behind at the dock. Fortunately, Trudy never showed even a little uneasiness in her facial expression. Occasionally, when he expressed to her his concern about the Korean mission, she would just keep her brilliant smile, saying, "I have faith in you."

In December of 1959, the ship roared a "booooom" as it anchored at the port of Pusan. The ship's main gate had opened, and the couple slowly walked out on the long gangway that had been lowered. At last, he stepped foot on home soil.

It was the return to his motherland—taking the first step toward evangelizing his homeland. It had taken him exactly eight years to return.

MOTHER AND AN AMERICAN DAUGHTER-IN-LAW

They had to spend the night in Pusan because the final boat had already departed north to Incheon. The next day, when they had finally arrived at the port of Incheon, an American missionary from the Evangelical Alliance Mission (also a Bob Jones graduate) had come out with a Land Rover to greet them.

Among the crowd, Billy noticed someone who looked like his mother! She appeared the same—her hair tied up and wearing her usual white Korean jeogori top. Yet her hair had traces of gray and her face was creased with wrinkles. Of course, he knew she had become a grandmother. But now he noticed that her facial cheekbones had become more defined and she had become frail and thin. His heart became pierced with pain.

Oh Mom! he thought. *You've gotten so old waiting for this unworthy son. I am so sorry. Please forgive this undutiful son.* He wanted to run as fast as he could and hug her and be hugged, but the heavy bags in both of his hands were dragging him down.

Not too far away, his mother's eyes met his. The edges of her eyes turned red as they began to fill with tears. She wiped her tears with a handkerchief, the same white handkerchief she had used to wrap goodies for him from a neighbor's party.

Now, she was only a few feet away. Unbelievably, "Mother" was standing before him. Billy was not an orphan anymore. He flung his bags to the ground, running and hugging his mother. "Mom, I came back alive!" he wanted to shout, but the lump in his throat made him unable to make a sound.

The tears he held in for the past eight years poured out. They cried together without a word. She was inside the arms of her youngest son, now grown as a man bigger than she—crying with tears of joy . . . and the sorrow she had held inside.

Only after profusely crying, did his mother notice her American daughter-in-law, Trudy. Without any formal introduction, instinctively, she knew that this was her daughter-in-law. Openly, and without any hesitation, she walked toward Trudy and hugged her in her arms.

Then, she cried some more. Her tears were a quiet "thank-you" for taking care of her son in a foreign land far away, as well as a heartfelt "thank-you" for Trudy's willingness to follow her son to this unfamiliar, impoverished country. Trudy, in return, had a peaceful smile as she hugged Billy's mother who was much shorter than she—below her shoulders.

Suwon was the same town he had left eight years earlier—impoverished and barren. The red fabric strips of the shamanistic temples were still hanging at the edge of town, still blowing in the wind.

Billy's thatched home of birth had not changed either. Time seemed to have stopped here. *There is so much to be done for my hometown and my homeland*, he thought.

Shortly after Billy's return, a rumor began about the couple, and especially Billy's American wife. "If President Seung Man Lee's wife, Franchesca, was wealthy enough to buy the entire Korean peninsula in a single purchase, Pastor Billy Kim's wife, Trudy, was so much wealthier that she would be able to purchase the entire peninsula, times three! They shipped seven boatloads of newlywed household goods!"

A NEW LIFE IN A THATCHED HOME

The proof of this, according to the rumor, was their Ford pickup truck. Having a car was truly a precious rarity, and so the idea of a "Rich Trudy" seemed very believable. Despite those false rumors, Billy and Trudy started their Korean life living in his mother's three-bedroom thatched house, as part of a large fourteen-member household: Billy's oldest brother and his wife, their nine children, Billy's mother, Trudy and himself. (Fortunately, the brother served in the Korean Army and often was away on duty.) The newlyweds would stay with Billy's family their first six months before he bought some adjoining land to build their own home.

However, the American daughter-in-law endured everything well. In fact, she thought the heated "ondol" floor was simply amazing and fun, and she played around on the warm flooring, rolling over and over. The fore-runner of American radiant heating via hot water or electricity, the ondol floor of the twentieth century channeled the cooking fire from the outside kitchen to heat up the stone and mud floors of the main house. Passage-ways directed the hot air and warm smoke underneath the main home before exiting the other side.[1]

As Billy kept himself busy preparing for the mission work in Korea, Trudy was learning Korean customs with her mother-in-law. Trudy smiled away the trying times—adjusting to her life in Korea, learning unfamiliar customs, and living with her in-laws. She was being trained to become a great Korean missionary.

EVANGELIZING AT HOME

The first goal in the Korean mission work was to evangelize Billy's family. First and foremost, Billy began to pray for the salvation of his mother. After her were his oldest brother and wife and their nine chil-dren; then the second older brother with his wife and their five children; then his older sister and her husband and their three children; and lastly, the third older brother with his wife and their three children. Altogether, there were twenty-four family members whom he had decided to start evangelizing.

It didn't take long for an opportunity to arise to share the gospel. His oldest brother suggested that they all go to their father's grave. They stood in front of the grave with a nicely prepared meal and wine. One by one, the family members bowed down to reminisce and pay respect to their late father.

"I cannot bow down to my father's grave," Billy said. Startled, confused, and barely able to calm his mind, the oldest brother asked for the reason.

Billy replied, "Because of Jesus." Billy shared about Jesus Christ in front of his father's grave to all of his family members. An awkward feeling of estrangement surrounded the grave during the family's visit.

Even so, there were some family members interested in this gospel, which they were hearing for the very first time. Among them, the third brother was the most interested. He had just lost his job and was wondering what to do next, and having heard the gospel seemed to have opened his heart. That night, he came to Billy and wanted to hear more about this Jesus.

As they shared together, their hearts began to warm toward each other. The Lord was gently healing his brother's hurts. That same night he accepted Jesus Christ into his life. This was the day that the Korean mission bore its first fruit.

Then God gave him another opportunity to share the gospel with his family. It was on the anniversary memorial day of his father's death.

THE MEMORIAL SERVICE

Billy reverently asked his oldest brother, "On this anniversary day of our father's death, please allow me to officiate in the Christian way. Then, compare it with the way you used to officiate it, and choose whichever you feel is better."

Fortunately, his oldest brother accepted this suggestion. Instead of the traditional ancestral commemorative rite, a memorial service was given.

God's words of "love one another" were shared, and prayers followed; he asked for the health of family members, their well-being, and blessings. Also, Billy offered a eulogy to commemorate their father and recall memories of his lifetime. The eulogy had been written by a skillful evangelist, whom Billy had asked for assistance in advance. Even to Billy, it sounded quite impressive.

After the memorial service, they ate the prepared refreshments as they talked about fond memories of their father. They shared one episode after another, and after a while, the entire family became deeply immersed in missing their father.

After that day, the oldest brother burned all three ancestral commemorative rite sites in the house. Those sites were symbolic of generations of the family's faith in them to bring luck or misfortune and prosperity or adversity.

The entire family gave up those ancestral rites and, over time, all accepted Jesus into their lives. Billy felt that his family's surrender of their beliefs in those ancestral rites was worth his entire calling and eight years of training. The fruit of evangelism was sweeter than the best of honey.

As the youngest son, Billy felt pure delight as his siblings turned to the living God and began to worship His Son, Jesus. The brother closest to him in age (just three years older), Joon Hwan, would be the first one to pray with Billy for his salvation. Billy's mother was the second member of the family to pray to receive the Lord Jesus as her Savior, and she often prayed that all of her grandchildren would marry genuine Christian believers.

Jesus told His followers before ascending into heaven, "You will receive power when the Holy Spirit has come upon you, and you will be my witnesses in Jerusalem and in all Judea and Samaria, and to the end of the earth" (Acts 1:8). Billy and his family's Jerusalem began at their father's commemorative site. For every Christian, evangelism should begin at home.

A HOMETOWN CHURCH

In his childhood, Billy never once went to a Christian church. He would not visit a church even during the common Christmas festive celebrations. But as soon as he arrived back in his hometown, he went around the area to look for churches. Suwon Central Baptist Church was the only Baptist church. In the United States, Billy had seen many Baptist churches. However, in Korea Baptist churches were rare.

Suwon Central Baptist Church was in such a deteriorated state that it could dissolve and close its doors at any time and seemingly not be missed. Its daytime worship service consisted of mainly seniors, who numbered less than a dozen. The main pastor, Pastor Sang Yup Choi, was so old that he could barely walk.

Billy decided to visit Pastor Choi, and he introduced himself as Pastor Billy Kim. Pastor Choi acted as if he had already heard about him and was surprised and happy to see him. He asked Billy to lead the coming Sunday evening service, the Wednesday service, and to take over the entire Sunday school.

Billy was at a loss, for the requests were so sudden. However, he felt he could not accept the request. Billy's interest was not in regular church ministry. His interest was in going all over the country to hold evangelistic gatherings.

During his six years of weekend evangelism in the United States, Billy felt strongly that God had confirmed him to be a touring gospel evangelist. His heart was already set on replying, "I cannot."

Even so, he was hesitant to coldheartedly refuse the pastor's request from a church he was planning to continually attend in the future. Pastor Choi gently grabbed his hands.

"Pastor Kim, please do not turn down this old man's request." His feeble hands were slightly trembling as he spoke. At that moment, Billy's heart was greatly moved by the Holy Spirit.

"I lack in many ways, but I will try my best to help."

On January 1, 1960, Billy began the work of his calling for the gospel as an associate pastor of Suwon Central Baptist Church. He did not yet foresee the plans God had in store for Suwon Central Baptist Church. His eyes were like those of Elisha's attendant, the willing servant of Elisha, who could not see God's provision for the prophet (see 2 Kings 6:14–17).

Like Elisha's servant who saw limited resources, Pastor Kim saw only a worn-out church building about to collapse and a congregation of twelve people, mostly seniors. Nothing was visually attractive. No sign or hint was given from God, either. Still, he could not refuse an elderly pastor's request from his same denomination. And so Billy Kim became a valued pastor at Suwon Central Baptist Church.

EVANGELIZING THE HOMETOWN, SUWON

Along with his church ministry, he diligently continued the missions work. After all, it was only natural that Billy continued, for he was an official missionary sent by the US ministry Christian Service. The purpose of Christian Service was to spread the gospel, to properly guide youth, and to support the rural farm churches. This was also Billy and Trudy's purpose in their Korean mission.

Christian Service, founded by Waldo Yeager, had formed to support Billy and Trudy in their mission to Korea. The rural country churches and marketplaces were a great outreach opportunity for Pastor Kim to spread the gospel. Yet every time he reached out to rural churches and held evangelistic meetings, the churches were not in a financial condition to hold such events. The people attending those meetings brought rice and meat as their contributions.

So Pastor Kim traveled all over the country, searching for and finding marketplaces called "Jangtu" (like a farmer's market), and diligently preached the gospel on the streets. Eventually missionaries from the Oriental Missionary Society, as well as Rev. J. B. Crouse, the US Slavic Gospel Association's Pastor Peter Deyneka, and many others joined him in the "Jangtu" market outreach. Pastor Crouse was good at singing hymns, and Reverend Deyneka was almost a professional on the trombone.

When the blue-eyed, foreign missionaries sang praises with the energetic sounds of the trombone, a lot of curious people gathered to see what was going on. When they went out for an evangelistic outreach in the Suwon area, many rushed to see the "wealthy" wife of Pastor Billy Kim. When the praises ended, Billy would begin his sermon.

"Only Jesus can deliver us from our poverty!"

"Only Jesus can save us!"

"I was only a US Army houseboy, but I met God, and now I have become a pastor before you!" He preached the gospel with a full, deep voice, as though the whole marketplace would be shaken. It seemed as though he would be content to die there, fervently sharing from his heart the gospel of the Lord Jesus.

The evangelism effort started to bear fruit. Especially in the Suwon area, a great number of students came to them. Most of them were students wanting to learn English from Billy and Trudy. The husband and wife team offered free English tutoring, and the offer gave the two an effective, natural method to present the gospel while teaching a second language. Trudy was the biggest help in this tutoring outreach.

In order to establish a systematic, organized Korean mission, the two realized they must set up a mission base. With the help of Christian Service, they were able to build a house to host guests (including students they would tutor) and seekers. The base house was roomy, comfortable, and built in the American style. However, the builders were nonprofessionals, so the house needed major repairs annually. For example, the Korean underfloor heating system had gaps, allowing briquette fumes to leak inside the house and causing the entire family to be hospitalized with gas poisoning seven times.

Their mission home suffered from more than faulty construction. On four different occasions thieves broke in and stole the mission funds. The electric gramophone they brought from America was stolen. Trudy had once directly faced the stealing intruders, making her heart nearly stop.

Despite a faulty building and at times primitive conditions, the Kims were happy and their missions home was always crowded with people. It was wonderful to share the gospel with the people who gathered. Most of the students there had been kicked out of their own houses for believing in Jesus, and they found a peaceful resting place at the base house.

HOSTING US AND KOREAN SOLDIERS

US soldiers at Osan Air Force Base heard about the missionary who married an American wife. The chaplain at the air base had Pastor Kim speak at the Sunday evening service once a month. After some attended the chapel services at the base, the soldiers decided to come to Suwon and visit Billy and Trudy's home and also attend the service at Suwon Central Baptist Church on Sunday morning. They had never visited a Korean church and were intrigued in visiting one. Before long, several men were invited to Billy and Trudy's home to enjoy having a meal with them. The meal usually was quite simple with cream of chicken over rice and homemade biscuits and canned corn and a simple salad and Korean kim-chee. Trudy even baked some apple pie and served ice cream for dessert with the piping hot pie.

Meanwhile Pastor Kim's ministry to soldiers included the Korean military. Eager to study English, some soldiers came to the English Bible study group called the "Good News Club" and studied the words of God along with English. Army soldiers listened to Pastor Billy Kim's English sermons, ate the delicious American home-cooked meals prepared by Trudy, and found comfort for their homesickness.

The base house was a small church. It was the mission center for the "Christian Service." It was where the weak became fulfilled as the body of Christ.

Billy's homeland was fast becoming evangelized, centered through the Suwon Central Baptist Church and the base house. Quietly, the foundational stepping-stones were being set in place for Korean evangelism and for world evangelism. Though unseen, the written promises of God were being accomplished: "Believe in the Lord Jesus, and you will be saved, you and your household" (Acts 16:31).

HOLD A
GRAND VISION

About six years after Billy became associate pastor of Suwon Central Baptist Church, he began to sense what God had in store for the church. Pastor Sung Yup Choi had begun to suffer from chronic illness, and it had become harder for him to walk. One day Pastor Choi, and later the entire congregation, asked Billy to become the main pastor of the church.

That night Billy fell prostrate in the church sanctuary. "Lord, what is Your will?" The Lord revealed to him an image of a worn-out and dilapidated church body. Warm tears ran down Billy's face. "Lord, I carelessly left aside Your body, the church."

At that very moment, he heard a roaring wind, like the voice of the Holy Spirit: "Rebuild My body!" Billy immediately purposed to obey God's command.

"Lord, I will take care of Your body, the church. I will rebuild this torn body of Yours."

THE GOSPEL OF LIFE GROWS

On January 1, 1966, Pastor Billy Kim became the main pastor of Suwon Central Baptist Church. After he accepted the position, he focused more on church work, while he continued his life calling of evangelism with passion.

Within eight months of taking leadership of the church, the registered congregation grew to three hundred members—becoming the largest church in Suwon. Most of the congregation consisted of students. Yet there were only about a hundred adult congregation members, and the calling to rebuild the church remained. Every day Billy knelt and prayed for the rebuilding of the church.

As he focused on the issue of rebuilding the church, a small but significant incident occurred. One day, two sisters, faithfully serving in the young adult group at the church, asked that he would come to share the gospel with their father, a notary public. Billy visited their father's home and earnestly shared the gospel for about thirty minutes. After hearing everything, their father, with a frown on his face, replied, "I do not wish to believe in God."

Billy didn't think much about it because it was a common response after hearing the gospel. He then asked, "Why do you think that way?"

"According to you, Pastor, it seems that God is truly a good God. Then why is it that the church building in which Christians serve your God is in such a deteriorated state and about to be ruined? How could such a God help me when I am having a hard time or when I get sick? I can never serve such a God who neglects the leaks in the roof of the church."

Pastor Kim felt a severe shock, as if hit with a big blow on the back of his head. He realized that God's heart for this issue was of great urgency. It seemed that God was not happy that he was dawdling with the cost of repairs. Returning to the church, he prostrated himself on the cold floor as if he was about to faint. The words of the father came back to him, piercing his heart like a sharp piece of glass.

"Lord, I will not make a visit to anyone until I rebuild this church." Billy decided to take a difficult stand. He envisioned hope instead of despair. A vision of a new church came to him. He heard the sounds of the congregation praising God and of children's laughter. Billy had felt faint; now his tightly clasped hands began to regain their strength.

"I will build a new church." The next Sunday morning, he openly declared his vision before the entire congregation. The people looked at each other and there was a buzz of talking. Immediately after the service, the head deacon ran toward him and demanded an explanation.

"With whom did you discuss this?"

God's voice was so clear in his ears that he had completely forgotten that he needed to ask the entire church's opinion and that a major decision like a new building must be made by the church committee.

"I'm so sorry. I discussed it with God." Billy explained the concerns he held in his heart regarding this issue. However, the head deacon was already against the idea, and with three other members he left the church. That head deacon had been so close, like a real brother. He had willingly given money to Billy to prevent him from having to sell his house.

A small mistake left a big scar. The pain Billy felt was like amputating an arm or a leg. He became greatly discouraged.

Once again, he knelt on the cold floor of the church. He raised his head and looked at the cross. Reminders of the Lord's pain came rushing to his heart. He firmly grabbed his chest and bowed on his knees. He now understood the Lord's heartache in seeing the ones He loved spitting and scoffing at Him. He knew his heartaches were incomparable to God's heartaches. A cool breeze blew over his face.

A NEW CHURCH: IT *CAN* BE DONE

Suddenly, he had an unexplainable peace. A courage that he had never experienced before rose up within him. As a boat sails to the seas of hope, he raised high his sails of courage. *It can be done.* He recalled the words in Philippians 4:13, "I can do everything through him who strengthens me," and knew it was God who would do it. He was simply a tool for God to use.

First, he requested help from the Southern Baptist Convention Mission Board. But the answer he received was no. Yet members of the congregation still wanted to tear down the small existing church. It was located on a high hill, and many knew how difficult it was for elderly members to climb to the church. It was decided that the hill could be leveled off and the new church could be more accessible if it were built on the level of the road running in front of it. That would add to the cost of a new building.

But the church members caught the vision, and they began to bring construction offerings. Many brought sacrificial gifts. One person sold his only prized possession, a solid gold wedding band. Some brought wristwatches that had been handed down from their fathers as family heirlooms. During that time, a watch was difficult to find, and it could be changed into cash quickly. US Army soldiers also took part in the construction offerings because Billy had led many of their worship services.

Pastor Kim and Trudy wrote to their friends in the US and described the sacrificial giving. Many of the Kims' supporters began to send a little extra each month for the building; they also told some of their friends about the need. The Kims sent pictures of the small and old building and mentioned that they were praying that it might be possible to build a little larger auditorium and take down the hill before starting the new building.

Within a couple of years the church had enough money to sign a contract with a reputable construction company.

When they took the first scoop with the shovel to start the rebuilding of the dilapidated old church, everyone shed overwhelming tears of joy. Later, during daily visits to the building site, Billy's face would become covered with dust, much the same as the construction workers. Meanwhile Trudy and other deaconesses were busy preparing meals to give to the workers. Students came as soon as their school hours ended, to help bring bricks to the building sites.

Adult church members, as soon as they got off work, would come to the construction site to help with anything possible.

As the bricks went up one by one, the people were overwhelmed, as if they were watching the very church of Christ being built. Everyone was of one mind and heart.

By May 1970, a beautiful two-story church building, with a seating capacity of six hundred, had been built and dedicated. Korean missions had taken another leap forward in the spread of the gospel.

Billy was convinced: "Sow the seeds of prayer. Water them with dedication. The One who makes them grow is God. The one who has life will grow. The gospel that changes lives also grows. The growth of the gospel must continue, until it reaches the ends of the earth."

SHALL I STAY? SHALL I GO?

Billy's evangelistic call outside Korea had begun just two years after he had returned to Korea. His Bob Jones alumni friends and other American friends did not forget the young Asian pastor, Billy Kim. Several churches invited him for their evangelistic conferences.

Korean missionary work was hectic and it remained on his heart, but he still made time to go back to the States for evangelistic meetings. He wanted to return the favor of having received knowledge of the gospel—and his spiritual salvation—in America. During 1970, invitations for him as the main speaker for international missions conferences began, not only in the United States but throughout Asia.

In 1970 and 1971 he would speak at major evangelism conferences in Colombo, Sri Lanka, and the Great Evangelism Conference in Hibiya Park of Tokyo, Japan. As Billy kept busy in Korea and throughout the world, with a great zeal for missions, a breakthrough occurred to increase the spread of the gospel.

On a warm spring day in 1973, a letter arrived from one of the world's largest evangelistic organizations—the Billy Graham Evangelistic Association (BGEA). Without any expectations, he opened the envelope. He thought that it was an official BGEA letter notifying Kim of Graham's plans to hold a crusade in Korea, which Kim knew the association had been planning for a year. He thought that it was merely an informational or support request letter.

"Pastor Billy Kim, we are writing to ask you to be the interpreter of the sermon messages of Pastor Billy Graham, in the coming Billy Graham Evangelistic Crusade in Seoul, Korea."

The words "Billy Graham" and "interpreter" passed through his vision and aroused many thoughts in his mind.

In 1957, while a student at Bob Jones University, Kim had attended a Billy Graham Crusade in New York. There, his vision of wanting to be an evangelist like Billy Graham began. In 1966, he had followed the

BGEA to Berlin, West Germany. As he had watched Billy Graham, he had dreamed of becoming a world evangelist. Moreover, two years prior, he had written a letter to Graham asking him to hold a crusade in Korea.

Billy Graham had been like a hero to him. That very evangelist was now asking him to be his interpreter in the Korea Crusade. There was no reason for hesitation. He should just accept the invitation and thank them for choosing him. It was an honor even to his family's name. It was surely a miracle that a former US Army houseboy had been selected to be an interpreter of Billy Graham's evangelistic messages.

BUT . . . BUT . . . BUT . . .

Choosing to be the interpreter for Billy Graham would mean giving up his love for his mother school, Bob Jones. Even during his college years, attending the Billy Graham Crusades had to be kept a secret. This was because the Bob Jones Academy and University schools strictly prohibited their students and their graduates from having anything to do with Billy Graham.

They reasoned that Billy Graham included as part of his crusades humanistic and liberal pastors. This was an unacceptable theological compromise. In addition, Bob Jones schools had branded the Billy Graham Evangelistic Association as being anticonservative in its Christian belief. Another reason behind this sensitive reaction was that Billy Graham himself had also studied at Bob Jones University, and he had brought several graduates of Bob Jones onto the crusade staff.

Indeed, Billy Graham and all names of Bob Jones graduates who were a part of BGEA were removed from the Bob Jones alumni records. If Billy took the role as an interpreter at the Billy Graham Crusade, he knew that his name would instantly be removed from the Bob Jones alumni records. Additionally, ten- and twenty-dollar monthly support from Bob Jones graduate friends and conservative churches would end.

To Billy, Bob Jones University was more than a mother school. He met God at Bob Jones for the first time. He dreamed his visions of faith there. He was trained there as an evangelist of the gospel. He was ordained there as a pastor. Bob Jones was the very foundational source of his faith. Bob Jones was like a source river of faith for Billy, and without it he thought he would not be able to take another step forward and would dry up. He could never give up Bob Jones.

Even so, giving up Billy Graham's interpreter role didn't seem possible either. First, it would pierce the heart of the conscience of his faith. *You said you wanted to become an evangelist like Billy Graham. You even sent a personal letter asking that Billy Graham hold a crusade in Korea. Why are you now avoiding it? What are you afraid of?* he asked himself.

There were other issues as well. Billy was a missionary sent to evangelize his homeland, Korea. He was well aware of what great evangelistic outcomes transpired through the Billy Graham Evangelistic Association and its large crusades. He had attended and witnessed it with his own eyes. Through the Billy Graham Crusade, he could imagine how much faster the evangelizing of his homeland could take effect. A missionary's personal situation was not to be compared with the evangelization of his homeland, he told himself. Yet still he struggled.

The BGEA had its own reasons for choosing Billy Kim to be the interpreter. After giving the gospel message, Billy Graham would invite people to come forward to confess their faith and to accept Jesus Christ as their Savior. This was the practice of Baptist churches but was unfamiliar to Korean churches. However, Billy was familiar with this method and had been trained for it in America. He could lead people in the time of confession and confirmation, better than any other Korean interpreter.

Also, interpreting for Billy Graham was more like giving a sermon than an interpretation, because people attending were going to be listening to the sermon from the interpreter, and not directly from Billy Graham. God might have put him through his strenuous speech training in high school to prepare him for this. This could be the reason why he had participated in so many roadside evangelistic meetings. This could be why he, from the very beginning of his ministry, had been given the opportunity to preach as the main speaker, at both Korean and internationally held evangelistic conferences and mission conventions. The Lord must have certainly, continually prepared Billy for this day.

A GREAT CONFLICT

A great conflict arose between his loyalty to his school and the opportunity to assist a visiting evangelist in his homeland.

I will not interpret.

I will.

Shall I stay?

Shall I go?

His heart had been tormented with the seemingly impossible decision he must make. He called Billy Graham's special aide and the chief director of the BGEA in Korea, Rev. Henry Holley. "Please give me forty-eight hours to respond."

"I will pray with you," was Reverend Holley's response. He was well aware of the difficulty Billy had in making this decision due to Kim's respect for and debt to Bob Jones University.

Placing the letter on top of the desk, Billy knelt on the floor. With his forehead to the ground, he called out for the Holy Spirit to help. Billy was unaware of the passing time.

He sensed the Holy Spirit quietly asking him, "Why are you here in Korea?" *I am here with the calling to evangelize my homeland.*

"Why are you avoiding it?" *It is because of my original source of faith— Bob Jones.*

"If you don't take the role . . . who can?" The Lord was asking him to walk the thorny path of reproach and expulsion from Bob Jones. He cried out from his heart.

It was then that God told him to lay down his prideful background— Bob Jones University. He was to renounce his pride and love of "Bob Jones." The result would be removing his name from the Bob Jones alumni. God wanted his pride and background to be only in God. God wanted him to be content in having his name recorded in the Book of Life. What God wanted was "Billy," not the graduate of Bob Jones, Pastor Billy Kim.

The Lord, in His own way, took him out of the spotlight of Bob Jones. At that moment, he was quietly alone and at peace before God. He stood there—without the Bob Jones masters in theology gown, without the American Baptist pastor's gown—as only a servant of God. Billy had decided to obey the Lord's command.

He called Pastor Holley. "I will accept the role of interpreter for Pastor Billy Graham!" He stood firm to march forward only for the growth of the gospel.

This is what he wrote in his diary on March 31, 1973: "My Lord has very clearly let me know what to do. After I decided to follow in obedience to His Word, I have found true peace in my heart."

PREPARING FOR GRAHAM IN KOREA

After Pastor Kim accepted the interpreter position, Pastor Holley immediately sent him Billy Graham's books, sermon notes, and actual videotapes of other BGEA crusades. Billy Kim had to become a Korean-speaking Billy Graham. People would hear him talk and shed tears of repentance. Through hearing the message spoken by him, they would come to dedicate their lives to God. He would prepare, and he recalled the painful training preparations he did as a high school sophomore at Bob Jones Academy to fix the "R" and "L" pronunciation for the speech contest.

Billy remained very busy with his work at the church, and the setup of the Asian broadcast, yet he took time to practice the accents, gestures, and intonations of Billy Graham. This was in addition to his efforts to help organize the crusade in Korea. He helped to arrange an opportunity for Pastor Holley to meet the highest leaders of the Korean society. He knew it required the help and interest of the government, heads of congress, military leaders, and the press in order to hold a successful evangelistic crusade.

BGEA's Pastor Holley was thankful for the preparation for Graham's meetings with cultural leaders as the crusade was under way, saying, "Billy Graham was able to have an official meeting with President Chung Hee Park and the leaders of the Korean society through the arrangements made by Pastor Billy Kim."

Planning had begun much earlier, based on the friendship of Billy Graham and Pastor Kyung Chik Han, of Youngnak Presbyterian Church. Their friendship began in 1951, when the Korean War was at its peak.

Billy Graham, after visiting the US Army front line, had preached to the crowds gathered in Pusan, and the interpreter then was Pastor Han. Their relationship grew when Pastor Han attended the Berlin Crusade in 1966 and asked that a crusade be held in Korea. The BGEA promised it would in 1972, but it was pushed back one year.

BILLY AND BILLY, SIDE BY SIDE

Pastor Kyung Chik Han, as the officiating host for the Korea '73 Billy Graham Crusade, raised the slogan Evangelize 50 Million Nationals. He predicted that there would be at least 200,000 attending every evening of the 1973 crusade and around 500,000 on the last day. However, attendance would go far beyond all predictions.

Prior to Seoul, Graham's six associate evangelists had led crusades in six other cities, with a total of 1.5 million people attending. Now Graham entered Seoul for a five-day crusade, from May 30 to June 3, 1973. On the first day of the Seoul meetings, held on the Yoido Island on the western boundary of the city, more than 300,000 people gathered. The Yoido People's Plaza was huge, but the crowds grew daily. On the final day, official records counted 1.1 million people filling the plaza.[1] It was the greatest number ever gathered at a single evangelistic event. In five days Graham had preached the gospel of Jesus Christ to a total of 3.2 million people —900,000 more than during the entire sixteen weeks in the New York 1957 crusade, and smashing the previous attendance record of 2.6 million in Glasgow in 1955.[2]

God made one nameless young man stand right in the middle of it all. Billy Kim looked stately on the right side of Billy Graham. The staff had placed a footstool for him to stand on. From the front of the podium, he did not look too short beside Billy Graham.

Standing in the center of the Yoido plaza, Kim thought of God's love and mercy placed on his life. His thoughts were of a great God's grace, that a shabby seventeen-year-old US Army houseboy could stand as the Lord's holy servant. The boy himself was simply useless. Everything was possible only by God's preparations, one by one, until that day. Briefly, he gave a thankful prayer.

Then Billy Kim's eyes captured the hundreds of thousands of people gathered in the square on the final day, along with hundreds of cameras from both local and international media broadcast and press. His throat felt so dry, as he prayed silently, "Lord, make me a Korean-speaking Billy Graham."

TWO VOICES AS ONE

At last, Billy Graham's powerful voice resonated throughout the Yoido People's Plaza, immediately followed by Billy's voice, pouring out to the more than one million people who had gathered. The two evangelists went back and forth naturally, in perfect sequence, like a trained athletic relay— preaching and interpreting.

The more time that passed, the more Kim's heart warmed to the message. His heart pumped faster by the minute, and he felt his heart might burst. The Holy Spirit was leading the two Billys' spirits together.

"Billy Kim actually enhanced Billy Graham," wrote Graham biographer John Pollock. "In gesture, tone, force of expression, the two men became as one in a way almost uncanny. A missionary fluent in Korean, who knew Graham personally, thought that Kim's voice even sounded like Graham's." Pollock noted that in the later rebroadcast in the United States, some TV viewers thought that Billy Kim was the preacher, and Billy Graham was the English interpreter.[3] At one point during the actual message, even Billy Kim got confused as to who was preaching. It felt as though he was preaching and Billy Graham was interpreting in English. The two seemed to be one.

Then Graham gave the invitation to accept Jesus as Savior. With more than one million crowded together, "He . . . made his invitation harder than usual. 'If you're willing to *forsake all other gods*, stand up.' There was a hush upon the audience at first. Then one here and one there arose, until thousands were standing."[4]

An amazing scene appeared right before Billy Kim's eyes. Dozens of people became hundreds, thousands became ten thousand . . . then a hundred thousand—all standing, raising their arms, tears of repentance on their faces as they came to God. Seemingly all of greater Seoul, with all types of people, was coming to God.

It was a historic moment for the Korean church—its first big step toward world missions. It was the hour that the Korean church took a big step forward for the gospel, and Billy stood in the middle of that great historical moment.

After the third day of the crusade, the weekly newspaper *Chosun*, which was known not to report any religiously related news, wrote of Kim: "Pastor Billy Kim did not merely interpret from English to Korean, but he completely digested the faith within Pastor Billy Graham's voice. His gifted speaking pierced the hearts of the crowds. It was that of a separate evangelist."[5]

Waldo Yeager of Christian Service was able to attend the Seoul Crusade. Afterward, he noted, "Billy Kim shared the gospel in his language with more people than anyone has ever done in history."

AFTER THE CRUSADE: KIM IN THE SPOTLIGHT

Afterward, the two Billys marveled at what they knew was a work of God. "The sheer fact of [the crusade] having gathered over three million people in five meetings with an additional million and a half conducted by my associates, makes it by far the largest face-to-face presentation of the gospel . . . in the history of the Christian church," Dr. Graham told the media. "This is the work of God. There is no other explanation."[6]

Kim told others after the crusade he had "a new vision, a new passion for the lost, and a new love for the Lord and His Word." One month later he wrote Graham, "I praise God for the influence you have had on my life personally."[7]

In the short term, however, the impact of the crusade would overwhelm the Korean evangelist. The flood of newspaper reporters from the first day of the crusade continued after the event, looking for interviews. On the first day after Dr. Graham left, Billy Kim was bewildered when he discovered that an interview was to be with him and not Billy Graham. When he realized that the interview had been posted as the headline on the following day, he was even more surprised.

Billy Graham should have been the one in the spotlight, and more than that, God should be honored most of all, not me, he thought. He wanted to escape from having the crowds interested in him. To a pastor, a desire for fame is the same as poison. He hurriedly contacted a friend, who was the head of a hospital, and requested to have a securely hidden room.

Trudy's heart was the same as his as she visited the hospital. "Billy, let's kneel and pray together for humility before the Lord," she told him.

Billy stayed there for a week, fervently praying with a humble, fearing heart. "Lord, remove any arrogant heart from me. Let only You, Lord, arise and be glorified."

Through prayer, Billy was able to keep a grand vision of his great Lord.

6

SPREAD THE GOSPEL WITH YOUR WHOLE LIFE

Within a month after the successful completion of the Billy Graham Crusade in Seoul, Billy received a letter from the president of Bob Jones University. "We have seen through overflowing news articles and pictures that you have compromised your position and cooperated with BGEA as you participated in the recent Billy Graham Crusade in Seoul."

From the first day of the crusade, the enormous crowds had caught the attention of America's major press and media and had been reported widely. "What we want from you," the letter continued, "is that you deny any prior relationships you had with Bob Jones University, and that you do not mention to anyone that you have been educated here. You are a disgrace to the school. You have gone against the principles set by the school and by which you were educated. We are no longer proud of you."

"Billy Kim" was removed from the list of Bob Jones University alumni. Billy was no longer invited to any events held with the name of Bob Jones University. He was forbidden from interacting with any of the alumni. If anyone from the school met with him, or was heard supporting him, they would also be eliminated from the rolls of Bob Jones alumni.

BEARING "THE CROSS OF BETRAYAL"

Of course, Billy was fully aware of what was going to happen, but when he actually read the letter, his heart was tormented. No matter how much he tried, he could not hold back the tears. Quietly, he entered his church and knelt down under the cross. The beautiful campus of Bob Jones flashed before his eyes. The sweet memories there passed through his mind. The pain he felt was as deep as the memories were sweet. He cried out for a long time as he knelt under the cross.

And then before his eyes a Jewish young man appeared. People gathered and threw stones at Him, saying, "Jesus! You're a traitor." Everyone had left Him. He went up the hills of Golgotha alone, carrying the cross.

Jesus spoke, as He looked down from the cross, "Billy, you have become a traitor too." Billy replied, "Lord, I've been branded as a cursed traitor by Bob Jones."

The Lord asked him, "Can you carry the cross of being a traitor?" It meant branding him with the shame of being marked as a "traitor." It was for him to be isolated from everyone. It was a lonely road. But then he suddenly realized, *Our Lord walked that path. He carried the cross of a traitor.* The secret of victory lay behind the cross of betrayal . . .

He realized the paradox of the cross that gives eternal life after death. "I will carry the cross of betrayal."

Billy, from that moment onward, decided to pray even more for Bob Jones University. He was determined not to be proud of "Billy Kim" but to be proud of "Bob Jones" more, and to further bless the school. He decided to pray that Bob Jones would become more tolerant, lenient, and forgiving within the truth. Decades later there would be a reconciliation between the school and the evangelist.[1]

After the removal of his name from Bob Jones alumni, God used Billy to an even greater extent. After the Billy Graham Crusade in Seoul, he began to be invited as the main speaker for large-scale revivals and evangelistic conferences internationally.

POWERFUL WORDS BY A HUMBLE EVANGELIST

In the 1980s and 1990s, two key conferences played a big role in making Billy Kim known as a world preacher and evangelist: the International Conference for Itinerant Evangelists and the Promise Keepers rallies. In 1986, the conference for evangelists was held in Amsterdam, Netherlands. Billy attended this event as the main speaker.

More than ten thousand gospel evangelists from 185 countries gathered to hear this Korean pastor. "We have received unconditional love from God. In the same way, we also need to give unconditional love to the people around us." As the sermon ended, all of the evangelists stood to their feet with passionate applause. The standing ovation lasted a long time.

The officiating host, Dr. Billy Graham, gestured with his hands for everyone to stop clapping and to sit down, but to no avail. Only when Billy Graham said, "Let's pray!" did everyone finally stop clapping.

After the assembly, a flood of interview requests came from reporters of many countries. One Swiss reporter asked, "Billy Kim, you are in the spotlight at this event. Why do you think God is using you in such a special way?"

In response to this, Billy replied, "I am not anyone special. Every one of the gospel evangelists gathered here are the special ones. I am merely a tool used for these special people. Do not focus your attention on me but on them."

When the reporter asked, "Are you satisfied with the sermon you gave today?" he replied, "No, I am not. I am still lacking in sharing the Lord's gospel, the good news."

Billy's longtime coworker, Pastor Jun Won Kim, manager of the Far East Broadcasting Company (FEBC) radio station in Daejeon, then told the reporter, "Pastor Billy Kim stays in his room fasting, praying, and meditating prior to giving any sermon for the day. He does this even when the sermon includes the same part about his childhood, and how he came to believe. It seems like he is giving his sermon not in front of the people but in front of God. I feel that is why Pastor Billy Kim is never satisfied with his sermon. It seems that he approaches even the very familiar parts of his sermons with a new heart of praise. He seems to always approach the podium as a place where he puts himself away and offers himself as a sacrifice."

Billy returned as the main speaker at the conference fifteen years later, at "Amsterdam 2000." His sermons in 1986 were recorded, together with their written texts. They are used as sermon curriculum in many American seminaries, even today.

MEN KEEPING PROMISES

The Promise Keepers movement started in America in 1990, with the vision of University of Colorado football coach Bill McCartney and his friend Dave Waddell to train men to demonstrate lives of integrity. One year later, 4,200 met in a University of Colorado arena. From this modest start, 22,000 men from every state gathered in 1992 at the school's football stadium and more than 50,000 male members the next year in the campus football stadium. After this, Promise Keeper conferences were held throughout America's major cities, in stadiums and grand convention centers, where tens of thousands of men gathered at each large venue.

Eight years after it was founded, in 1997, Promise Keepers held a gathering in Washington, D.C., called "Stand in the Gap." One million men attended, and the event received worldwide news coverage. They filled much of the National Mall for "six hours of standing and kneeling in prayer, worship, confession, repentance, and declarations."[2] In Korea, a special correspondent on MBC-TV reported on the event. Billy Kim was one of the major speakers.

Promise Keepers challenged Christian men to live godly lives and encouraged them to keep seven promises:

1. I will live a God-centered life.
2. I will live spreading the good news to my friends.
3. I will live keeping my purity.
4. I will live protecting my family.
5. I will live wholeheartedly serving the church.
6. I will live united with brothers in Christ.
7. I will live loving my neighbors.

In 1996 and 1997, Billy became the main speaker at PK conferences in Atlanta, Chicago, Honolulu, and Los Angeles. Between 40,000 and 70,000 men attended those weekend gatherings. The crowd clapped hard and long during each sermon by Pastor Kim. At the end of each Kim message, men were asked to stand if they wanted to vow to "pray once a day for their family, for the church they belonged to, and for their pastors." At each event, tens of thousands of men instantly stood in their seats.

A POWERFUL HANDSHAKE

Billy received such great responses from the audiences that he became one of the main speakers of Promise Keepers. Here is what Stanley Sebastian Jr., a Detroit businessman who accompanied Billy,[3] observed after Chicago's PK conference: "Billy Kim, after speaking to tens of thousands of men, and receiving frenzied applause, walked out of the stadium to go to his ride. On his way out, he walked toward a black American gentleman who was cleaning there and said to him, 'God bless you.'"

Dr. Kim had walked toward that custodian and offered a handshake. That black gentleman was so surprised he didn't know what to do. This speaker, who had spoken to thousands of men at Chicago's Soldier Field and received rousing cheers and heated applause, now wanted to shake the janitor's hand.

Sebastian said that the gentleman probably would never forget that moment and perhaps could receive Jesus as his Savior as a result of that incident. The businessman realized that Billy not only loved the crowds of people gathered there but also cared about and loved every individual person. It seemed as though Billy knew that a simple handshake could be the starting point of leading an individual soul to Christ.

THE EVANGELIST AS AN ACTIVIST AND AMBASSADOR

The president of the Baptist World Alliance (BWA) had normally been chosen from European countries and the United States. It was merely a dream for a colored race, an Asian pastor, to hold this position. That dream became a reality for Billy Kim in January 2000, when the eighteenth BWA General Convention in Melbourne, Australia, elected him as president. At that time, Korean President Dae Jung Kim was elated and sent a congratulatory telegram, saying, "We open the first year of the twenty-first century with your inauguration as the president of the Baptist World Alliance, and I truly congratulate you."

His five-year term as the president began with an official inauguration scheduled that July in Havana, Cuba (see introduction). In his inauguration interview with the worldwide press, Billy mentioned that he would try to pay close attention to neglected regions of the world. He noted that he was a pastor from the only divided nation in the world. He shared his strong desire for North Korea's religious freedom, his concern for human rights efforts, and especially for the North Korean refugee issues. Billy would emphasize these issues throughout his tenure as BWA president.

In March 2002, during the BWA executive committee's meeting held in Birmingham, England, and after hearing the report on the actual state of North Korea from Dr. Denton Lotz, general secretary of BWA, he discussed devising and adopting a BWA resolution toward securing international social standing of North Korean refugees. Along with discussions about detailed ways to help North Korean children and the infirm elderly, he sought ways to establish international-level support for human rights and religious freedom for North Korea. Three months later, during the BWA General Council meeting held in Spain, he laid out the foundational draft of those plans.

In 2003, during another BWA General Council meeting held in Korea, the request for the United Nations resolution granting North Korean escapees an international refugee status was adopted and handed to the UN, the United States, China, and other countries.

He also visited Russia, Ukraine, Poland, and other former communist countries to discuss their religious freedom and human rights issues. President Kim met with Poland's president, Aleksander Kwaśniewski, asking him to discuss religious freedom and human rights issues with the president of Kyrgyzstan, during the Kyrgyzstan and Kazakhstan Summit Conference. Poland's president formally agreed to do this.

Shortly after the devastating April 22, 2004, train explosion in Ryongchŏn, North Korea,[4] Billy Kim met with the East European religious leaders, highlighting the status of Korea's divided country. He pointed to the growth and development of the Korean churches and to North Korea's current situation. He also vividly related the heart-wrenching, tragic stories of the Ryongchŏn explosion and asked for their prayers. He emphasized that only through prayer can the world's many disastrous and difficult situations be resolved.

During a visit to Romania, Kim met with government officials and received a promise in support of his cause for North Korea. In Bulgaria, he met with religious and political leaders, petitioning them for Christian support for Ryongchŏn's terrible tragedy. This resulted in an active promise of help from Bulgaria's leaders. The local Korean newspapers reported that Pastor Billy Kim was the first ever to request prayers and support for the devastated people of Ryongchŏn's accident by visiting East European countries as a Korean Christian leader.[5]

In addition, as the president of BWA, Billy frequently visited the conflicted regions of Israel and Palestine, earnestly carrying out the role of an evangelical ambassador of the gospel of peace. He was in the forefront in supporting the sending of relief goods and foods to Kosovo, Ethiopia, India, Mozambique, and North Korea.

He also had the responsibility to care for all the Baptist churches of the world and to hold conferences in regional churches to spread the gospel, but Billy never stopped his diligence in spreading the gospel of the good news in Korea. One prime example was that he baptized around four thousand soldiers while they were on active field duty at the army training base camp in Choongnam.

Billy would always get up early in the morning to start the day with prayer no matter where he was in the world. Former vice president of FEBC-Korea, San Woong Min, recollects:

Whenever we went on a business trip for official work or to lead a conference, I would always share a room with Pastor Billy Kim. It was arranged this way to cut down on expenses. Once we had an opportunity to visit the US together. On that trip we shared a room as usual, and I was awakened in the early morning hours. Pastor Billy Kim had quietly gotten up and taken his Bible with him to the bathroom. What

I saw through the crack of the bathroom door that early morning was truly admirable. He had closed the lid of the toilet and sat there for a long time, reading his Bible and then praying until the bright hours of the morning. He had flown over ten hours the previous night and had no opportunity to adjust to the time difference, so it should've been really hard for him to do that. Honestly, I thought to myself, no one is looking, so why bother? Pastor Kim lives as if he is always before God.

THE EVANGELIST WHO PREPARES OTHERS

Billy, until he turned seventy years old, lived as if driven by a windstorm. Even in such a busy life as his, there were times when he needed a good night of rest. In 2004, Billy decided to retire as the main pastor of Suwon Central Baptist Church. The Baptist church did not have a formal retirement age, but he wanted to retire, following the customs of other Korean churches, and to carry out his dream of nurturing the next generation of God's servants.

The church that started with ten members had grown to more than fifteen thousand members. The church building had to be rebuilt again to accommodate such a large congregation. He hoped that a younger pastor with even greater ability would take over the church and grow it to an even larger church. Some social media communities rumored that one of his sons would take over the church. In spite of all the rumors, Billy, when others close to him were furious and told him to refute such claims, simply said, "Time will tell."

However, the pastor to succeed him was selected after all possible candidates had a fair chance to give a sermon. The names of the candidates were listed alphabetically, and the congregation voted. The new pastor chosen, with more than 90 percent vote of approval, was Pastor Myung Jin Ko. Pastor Ko had served Suwon Central Baptist Church as an assistant pastor for eleven years and was a spiritually powerful pastor. Previously under his leadership, the Osan Baptist Church had grown three times larger within a short period. He was kind natured, with an ability to warm the hearts of others.

At forty, the young pastor took charge of the existing church. It felt as though the church had become fresh, like the flutter of a young trout. When he retired, the Suwon congregation honored their senior pastor, Billy Kim, and he vowed to become a strong support for his successor and to assist him to grow into a great pastor.

In July 2005, BWA held a centennial celebration at the International Convention Center of Birmingham, England. During the centennial conference, Kim successfully completed his five-year term as president. Korean president Moo Hyun Roh sent a congratulatory telegram, saying, "Pastor Billy Kim has worked so hard all this time for the world's peace and human rights issues, and I trust he will continue to do even greater things."

Twenty thousand people from 107 countries gathered in London, birthplace of the Baptist World Alliance, making it the largest of all the BWA conferences. England's Pastor David Coffey was elected as the succeeding president.

As outgoing president, Billy spoke emphatically. "We must approach nonbelieving people with the everlasting truth by means of today's various methods. The fact that you and I are here today is definitely not by coincidence, and our Lord prepares everything for us."

At a commemorative service of appreciation two months later, Billy's longtime fellow servant of God, Pastor Yong Gi Cho of Yeouido Full Gospel Church, remarked in his sermon, "Pastor Billy Kim is the pride of the Korean Christian community, and a gigantic pillar in the world's Baptist Alliance, through his role in leading the world's Baptist churches since 2000. He has also contributed to raising the standing of Korea within the international community. The Korean churches applaud and congratulate you. Pastor Kim—a man of vision, a man of faith, and a man of love—will continually do greater works in God, and we will all pray to our Lord that it will be so."

In response, Billy turned the praise toward God. "Greatest admiration and glory to God in the highest who has led me thus far, though I am lacking, and I bow my head in sincere gratitude for those partners in faith who have supported me until this day along with their prayers. In the days ahead, until I go to meet Him in heaven, I will strive with all my heart and body to do any work for God."

LIFE IN "RETIREMENT"

After his retirement as president of the BWA, in November of that year until February of the next year, Billy traveled across the United States twice, holding large evangelistic conferences, each lasting over ten days.

In May 2006, he was invited to give the sermon for the graduating commencement ceremony of the US Air Force Academy, through the request of the US Air Force command chaplain, Charles Baldwin. It was the first time for an Asian to have this honor.

The following summer, July 13, 2006, he held a large evangelistic conference at the World Cup Stadium in Seoul with the well-known pastor and author Rick Warren of Saddleback Church in California. In 2005, the head of the department of broadcasting standards and regulations at the Far East Broadcasting Company, Yong Ho Kim, suggested FEBC invite Pastor Rick Warren to hold a seminar for pastors as part of its upcoming fiftieth anniversary. He suggested this because Rick Warren's book *The Purpose Driven Life* was selling in Korea by the hundreds of thousands. Now Pastor Warren reciprocated their friendship by speaking at the Seoul Olympic Stadium event.

The rain that had poured all day and had been forecasted to continue suddenly stopped just two hours prior to the event. Despite the wet roads, paths, and even seats, 100,000 people gathered. The number of people was more than the stadium could hold, so they put up several gigantic video screens outside the World Cup Stadium. The audience sat on the grounds and in the stands, uncomplaining, until the late hours of the night, listening to Pastor Rick Warren's preaching, which was interpreted by Billy's son, Pastor Joseph Kim.

After this, Billy visited Tokyo to hold an evangelistic conference. He also officiated at the morning prayer of the Korean-Japanese Christian Assembly Members Federation. He visited the national troops camp in Jaitoon to comfort the soldiers stationed there and held an evangelistic conference in Jakarta, Indonesia.

Later he would meet with the president of Guatemala, the prime minister of Cambodia, and the secretary general of the UN, Ki Moon Ban. In each instance he requested their help and cooperation for the region's missionaries, as well as support for the impoverished and neglected nations.

AN AMBASSADOR OF GOODWILL
AND THE GOSPEL IN CAMBODIA AND MONGOLIA

On November 23, 2009, the government of Cambodia invited Pastor Billy Kim to receive its highest honor, the National Assembly Medal, presented to a person who had the most significant impact in foreign relations, business achievement, or politics. Most striking was that a Buddhist nation—Cambodia is 90 percent Buddhist—would honor a Christian pastor and a foreigner.

On the day of the honor, the prime minister attended the event personally, presenting the medal to Kim and showing his appreciation and friendship. Billy's love for Cambodia began in 2006, by facilitating a donation of 5,000 self-generating electrical radios, worth about $65,000. Kim had received a notice from Prime Minister Hoonsen about Cambodia's urgent need for defense against natural disasters. After this, he was able to facilitate support with relief goods, like the radios and other items. He gave soccer balls to the Cambodian national soccer team as a gift and arranged an invitation for them to come to Korea for a soccer match, standing at the forefront of cultural exchange between the two nations.

In this way Billy had become an ambassador of goodwill. God moved the leader's heart of that nation to make it possible for a large evangelistic conference. It was a surprising opportunity to present the gospel in Cambodia.

Similar to this was "the miracle of Mongolia." Vice Prime Minister Sokahn and many Mongolian government officials had attended the conference in Cambodia and heard the good news of the gospel. After his return, the vice prime minister gave his support in promoting gospel meetings in Mongolia. Missionaries there were able to start many new churches. Central Baptist Church in Suwon was instrumental in starting twenty new churches in Mongolia.

AN ACTIVE RETIREMENT

When Pastor Kim retired as the main pastor of the Suwon Central Baptist Church and as the president of the Baptist World Alliance, he thought he would have a lot of time on his hands. However, that was not God's plan.

God spoke to Billy. "Walk this path throughout the days of your life until the hereafter!"

Not long after, his son Joseph, who dreamed of doing team pastoring after he had seen a successful model in the Chicago area while attending seminary, decided to begin a small church, Won-chon Church. If the number passed three hundred people, including children, the church would call another pastor and divide that church and continue like that. Antioch Church is the outgrowth of the Won-chon Church. Joseph asked his father to pastor the members who were over fifty in the Antioch Church. Today that church has five hundred members in their fifties, sixties, and seventies.

Thus Billy began his second life of ministry. From time to time, Billy had held three-day evangelistic meetings in different churches around Korea. Now retired, rather than doing all three days of revival meetings himself, he decided that his two preacher sons should each take one of the nights. The three pastors together toured the country, speaking about the parable of the prodigal son in Luke 15. The messages of the three pastors became known as "The Sermons of the Three (Father-Sons) Musketeers."

The younger son, Pastor John Kim, spoke about the "heart of the prodigal son"; the elder son, Pastor Joseph Kim, spoke of the "heart of the eldest son"; while Pastor Billy Kim spoke about the "heart of the father." There couldn't be any retiring from the calling to share the gospel.

Billy continues to arise in the early hours of the morning to start his day in prayer. If there is a sudden opportunity to share God's Word with anyone, he rises immediately and goes. He moves diligently to wherever his help is needed. Though his official term to work has ended, he is asked to come to many places and has many people to meet and many things to do.

His busy schedule is mostly related to sharing the gospel. Even when his schedule does not directly include presenting the gospel, he always tries to include the gospel message. The calling for the gospel will never cease until the end of his life. Billy's work for the calling will never cease, until the moment he stops breathing!

Billy may never see the day that he could really sleep late, until the day he is eternally at rest. Still, he is happy every day. Day by day, more and more, his heart is freshly renewed in the calling for the spread of the gospel. His goal and energy reflect those of the apostle Paul, who wrote to the Ephesians: "However, I consider my life worth nothing to me; my only aim is to finish the race and complete the task the Lord Jesus has given me—the task of testifying to the gospel of God's grace" (Acts 20:24).

Billy is a happy gospel evangelist. He will walk all the days of his life until the hereafter, step-by-step, for only one purpose—that of spreading the good news of the gospel.

Houseboy Billy Kim with an American soldier (top left) and with Sergeant Carl Powers. Billy visits Sergeant Powers's home in Dante, Virginia, during his first year in America.

THE FUTURE TEACHERS OF AMERICA

Billy, top right, poses with classmates at Bob Jones Academy. College freshman Billy Kim and fellow student admire bust of General George Washington at Bob Jones library. Billy with his college roommate, Jerry Thompson.

Bridesmaids prepare
Trudy for the wedding.
The newly married Mr.
and Mrs. Billy Kim depart
the church and afterward
enjoy wedding cake at
their reception.

Trudy Kim looks toward shore, about to leave Long Beach, California, bound for Korea and a new ministry with her husband. In Korea she draws close to her mother-in-law (with the Kims' first two children, Joseph and Mary Kay), and begins to raise their own family while Billy develops his ministry as a pastor and evangelist.

Billy Kim began his pastoral ministry in 1960 as associate pastor at the small Suwon Central Baptist Church. Twenty-five years later Pastor Kim preaches in the new sanctuary. After the service, he greets many who packed the church on celebration Sunday.

A packed Sunday morning service. Afterward Pastor Kim pauses as he and other Central Baptist Church leaders greet worshipers. The pastor, teacher, and evangelist has his well-worn Bible and sermon notes in hand.

After his retirement as pastor of Suwon Central Baptist Church, Dr. Kim would join his two sons, John (left) and Joseph, and preach the story of the prodigal son during three-day revival meetings throughout Korea (see chapter 6).

Billy Graham addresses the media after arriving in Seoul for his 1973 crusade, as Ruth Graham and Billy Kim listen. Pastor Kim translates each of Graham's messages during the five-day crusade. As Dr. Graham preaches in Yoido Plaza, photographers move about the stage and Kim waits to translate.

At the final service of his Korea '73 crusade on June 3, Billy Graham preaches to 1.1 million people at Yoido Plaza, the largest live audience for an evangelistic message. During the five-day crusade, more than 3.2 million attend the meetings.

Evangelist Kim preaches at daylight rallies in Seongnam, outside Seoul, as well as nighttime rallies in Incheon (opposite page, top) and Seoul.

Beginning in the 1970s, Pastor Kim led evangelistic rallies. One of the earliest, in his hometown of Suwon (then Suweon), featured a parade, musical talent, and a colorful stage.

Evangelistic rallies held indoors create intimacy and surround guests with color, here in Jeju (top) and Suwon.

Billy Kim speaks to evangelists from around the world at the Second International Conference for Itinerant Evangelists, better known as Amsterdam 86. Pastor Kim would speak again to the evangelists at Amsterdam 2000.

Pastor Kim speaks in US stadiums in 1996 and 1997 as part of the Promise Keepers movement. In five cities, including Atlanta (top), Honolulu (middle), and Washington, D.C., he challenges men to be spiritual leaders.

A billboard advertises the Billy Kim mission to Mongolia. Pastor Kim wears native coat while preaching in Mongolia. Earlier he preached in a stadium in Cambodia.

Part 2

THE ECONOMIST
LEAVING A FIVE-TALENTS PROFIT

Jesus told the parable of the five talents, in which a master gave three servants different amounts of money to care for (Matthew 25:14–28). When he returned, two had multiplied what they had received, but one merely buried it in the ground. The one with the greatest number of talents—five—returned it all, with five more! God has given us valuable talents, both monies and abilities, to invest in His work.

Your gifts and mine ought to be used to honor God—whether you are a pastor or a staff worker. Among the ways we can invest in His work are to value people and save money (chapter 8), manage our talents according to godly principles as well as give money and time to advance His kingdom (chapter 9), and partner with and assist others to multiply the impact of His kingdom (chapter 11). Being called as a good steward not only means diligently gathering and saving. It also means diligently sharing. In part 3 we will see these principles and more in action.

GRAB HOLD OF THE GOD-GIVEN CHANCE

7

I n May 1970, though it was spring in Suwon, the air of the early mornings was often quite chilly. On such a morning, after his usual early prayer time, Billy started his car and drove to a breakfast prayer meeting, which Korean President Chung Hee Park would attend as well. As he got out of the car, the president's bodyguards ran over to him to make certain of his identity.

Billy had only been in Korea for ten years and was a young pastor in his thirties. It was highly unlikely for him to be invited to attend the president's breakfast prayer meeting. The reason he went there that day was to interpret for a foreign guest speaker who had been invited. After finishing the interpretation for the speaker, he sat down at his breakfast seat. A Western-looking person approached him, looking as if he knew Pastor Billy. Billy did not immediately recognize him.

"Hi! I'm Wilkinson." It was David Wilkinson, his fellow alumnus of both the Bob Jones Academy and University. They had been close friends during their school years. They had gone together to roadside evangelistic outreaches and even secretly attended the school's prohibited Billy Graham Crusade in New York. Now more than a decade later, they renewed acquaintances.

LEARNING ABOUT THE
FAR EAST BROADCASTING COMPANY

David Wilkinson was working as the Japanese branch manager of FEBC (the Far East Broadcasting Company). FEBC had been founded in December 1945 as a radio broadcast for the purpose of China missions by US Army First Lieutenant John Broger, Pastor Robert (Bob) Bowman, and William Roberts.

The two Bob Jones alumni hugged each other and shared fond memories of college days. Toward the end of their friendly talk, Wilkinson asked Billy for some help. He asked for help in relocating the FEBC radio transmitting base from Okinawa, Japan, to Jeju Island, Korea. Wilkinson described the FEBC situation, and soon Kim would realize the urgency.

Wilkinson quickly summarized details of what had happened to the broadcasting enterprise. During its initial founding, FEBC had asked the Chinese national government, which was having serious internal conflict, for permission to set up a radio transmitting base. The government denied the request, so leaders decided to establish their transmitter in the Philippines. There FEBC initiated its China missions broadcast. A short time later mainland China became a communist nation, making the ongoing broadcasting imperative for the cause of China missions. FEBC relocated its transmitting base in 1957 to Okinawa, which was under US jurisdiction. They set up a studio base in Hong Kong.

However, in 1968, the United States began diplomatic negotiations to return Okinawa to Japan. As the time came near for the reversion of Okinawa, the Japanese government requested that the FEBC radio transmitter in Okinawa be removed. The Japanese government's reason behind the request was that transmitting a Christian missions broadcast, which the communist Chinese government did not want, could possibly jeopardize Japan's future relationship with China. Now FEBC was searching for a suitable location to move its base. Jeju Island, forty miles south of the Korean mainland and one of South Korea's nine provinces, seemed an ideal site because of its regional location.

Wilkinson was asking Billy to help FEBC relocate their broadcast base station to Korea. Billy knew nothing about broadcasting, but he remembered something he had heard during a dinner with some people who worked at a broadcasting company. Someone had said, "In Korea, it's easier to change a man into a woman than to get legal permission for a broadcast station."

Billy was an ordinary pastor of a small rural church in Suwon. Although having a graduate degree in theology from the United States provided opportunities to become an interpreter for various events, he had no connections with government officials to help Wilkinson set up the radio station. The request seemed almost laughable.

Still, he could not coldheartedly refuse his longtime friend. What Wilkinson was trying to do was vitally important for China missions. This was to spread the gospel! He wanted to help Wilkinson.

"I will try my best." Billy didn't realize what a great impact that one sentence would have later in his life. He didn't realize that it was a calling from God. He simply had the heart to help a friend who was trying so hard to share the gospel of God.

REALIZING A SUMMONS

"Lord, what should I do?" While thinking about Wilkinson's request the following morning, he knelt under the cross inside his church. During his prayer, Dr. Chi Young Yun came to mind. Dr. Yun was the head of the Republican Party in Korea and was in government authority. Billy had interpreted for Dr. Yun when he was giving a speech to major foreign officials and had remained close with him from that occasion.

He rushed to pay Dr. Yun a visit. "Head Representative, sir . . . please help us set up a base for a missions broadcast station." Billy's voice was firm and more determined than at any other time. He did not hesitate before Yun, for this was not a personal request but one for the work of God. He quickly summarized the situation related to the FEBC broadcast station.

Dr. Yun replied, "In order to overcome communism, I've always thought a missions broadcast is better than an army division. I will try to help as much as I possibly can."

Billy never thought in a million years that setting up a broadcast station would help to oppose communism. He could sense God's direct intervention in the work.

Dr. Yun then introduced Congressman Ik Jun Kim, who could help him directly. Congressman Kim was an elder at the well-known Saemunan Church and had a reputation as a bulldozer. Without another word, he raised both arms to signal his unconditional help. There were a lot of people to meet, many departments to visit, and piles of documents to obtain various permissions.

CHALLENGE AFTER CHALLENGE

Even if Kim was fortunate enough to receive a permit from the government, that would be only the beginning. He had to get permission from the World Conference on International Telecommunications because of the effects of radio frequency transmitting to nearby countries. This was not an easy matter considering that the nearest country, Japan, would be receiving a strong frequency output. Japan had already informed them about how uneasy they were about this issue.

Korea, Japan, China, the United States, and the Soviet Union (Russia) had been dealing with delicate tensions among their countries. The more Billy went back and forth from Korea to other countries, going from one department to another, running here and there for the documents, the more his mind told him that "setting up a broadcast station" would be plainly impossible!

Billy was just helping out a friend, whereas, imagine the actual person in charge of the relocation. Wilkinson's hardship was beyond words.

HELP IN HIGH PLACES

However, major help came from an unexpected source. FEBC needed to know where to purchase the land for the broadcast station. For this, the chief of staff for ROKAF (Republic of Korea Air Force), General

Man Ho Ock, made a significant contribution: He loaned an eight-passenger aircraft to survey the broadcast station's ground site from the sky. Use of a plane became a vital tool in searching for the perfect location.

General Ock had been a personal acquaintance of Billy's since 1962, when Ock had been the commander of Suwon's 10th Fighter Wing. During that time, Billy had led the worship of the 10th Fighter Wing, and Trudy had taught the officers' wives English. The two couples had become close during that time.

As a result of surveying for the best location with the air force private plane, they came to the conclusion that Jeju Island would be the ideal site. Soon they discovered that the selected land was owned by forty-three people. If just one person refused to sell the land, building the broadcasting station on that site would face a difficult obstacle. Billy visited each of the landlords, trying to convince them. It was not an easy task, but time and time again, appropriate people showed up to assist.

On February 11, 1971, the entire site was purchased under the name of the broadcasting station, and they finished recording the legal registration documents. Nothing could compare with the joy David and Billy felt.

On that day, they both stood on the promised site, as they envisioned the gospel of the good news being transmitted to the lands of North Korea, China, and even to the far regions of Russia. The two men visualized the comfort the persecuted and oppressed believers of communist countries would receive as they worshiped in their underground churches. They visualized God's children raising their hands high, as they turned back to God from the ends of the world.

Both stood for a long while looking toward northbound missions in tears, deeply overwhelmed and grateful. Yes, many things still needed to be processed to receive permission for an actual broadcast station. But now they had purchased the land, and their hearts were afloat, thinking that the radio station would soon open.

GOODBYE, DEAR FRIEND

Then, one August morning, a totally unexpected phone call deeply pierced Pastor Kim's heart. "Wilkinson is dead."

It was a call from Eun Young Oh, his secretary. Overwork was given as the reason. Billy fell to the floor. He gazed endlessly at the ceiling. Suddenly, agonizing tears came to his eyes, as he realized his mistake of not taking care of his friend's health. He walked back into the empty sanctuary, weak in his legs, and fell prostrate on the floor.

"Billy, thank you! Thank you!" He could still see Wilkinson, as if standing before him, saying, "Thank you!" over and over, with the biggest smile on his face for every small task accomplished.

"Farewell . . . Wilkinson!" Wilkinson's death not only brought the sorrow of losing a good friend but also the bigger task of establishing the broadcast station by himself.

ANOTHER EVANGELISTIC CALLING

He knelt down in deep prayer. "Lord, what should I do?"

"Preach the gospel to the ends of the earth." God was ordering him to continue, until the establishment of the FEBC broadcast station would be finalized.

"Lord, I will transmit the gospel of the good news to the ends of the world." At that very moment, Billy knew God had given him the task of establishing the Far East Broadcasting Company in Korea. It was a calling from God. At last, Billy realized his summons to the missions broadcast.

Later, FEBC Council Chairman Bob Bowman would recollect,

I came to know, through God's divine providence, the great Korean evangelist, Billy Kim. He was already busy with his daily missionary responsibilities. When I first met him, Billy told me that he was absolutely willing to help arrange the contacts with the Korean government, for permission to establish the broadcast station. Billy had not yet realized that God had chosen him to lead the work of radio broadcast missions. However, not long after, he understood the great task God had placed on him.[1]

After the death of David Wilkinson, Billy suddenly became the person in charge of establishing the FEBC broadcast station on Jeju Island. He was already busy with missions work, inside and outside Korea. Even so, he flew both in and out of the country repeatedly, trying to establish the broadcast station in heartfelt obedience to God.

THE QUEST FOR THE BROADCAST STATION

Congressman Ik Jun Kim had an essential role in obtaining permission for the broadcast station. Every time permission was needed, Congressman Kim accompanied Billy, charging into that particular department's office to obtain it. Of course, usually they would make appointments and wait for a response from each department. As visitors, they also displayed good manners. However, they just did not have enough time to always use gentlemanly methods.

"Sign this document, please!" They may have made an appointment, but Congressman Kim often entered the departments without knocking, handing workers a document to sign, sometimes with a loud voice, as if Billy and he were collecting a debt. Billy didn't know where the congressman got the courage.

Sometimes they entered an office without an appointment, resulting in receptionists bustling about and confused department representatives wondering who they were. Yet, remarkably, everything always went forward.

When Congressman Kim and Pastor Kim faced difficulties, God always sent the needed people to help. Obtaining the permit, which had seemed nearly impossible, was moving toward completion. At times it felt as though all they needed to do was pass each department, one after another, with the documents. It was clear that God was directly paving the way.

The dream of opening the new broadcast station was approaching reality. The headquarters of FEBC wanted to name it the "Far East Broadcasting." However, "Far East" in Korean would be "Keuk Dong," and "Keuk Dong Broadcasting" was already used by TEAM Missions. As a result, FEBC decided on the next best name: "Asia Broadcasting."

The facility was finally complete, and a trial broadcast was scheduled for April 30, 1973. However, one task remained. The radio transmitter needed to pass customs before even a trial broadcast could take place.

The radio transmitter had arrived at the Pusan port a full year previously, but the high fee required by customs had become a problem. FEBC's financial condition made it impossible to pay the customs charge. As time passed, the storage cost also continued to increase.

After many efforts at getting a customs tax exemption, Billy Kim spotted a good opportunity. Former US president Harry Truman had just died, and Korea's Prime Minister Jong Pil Kim would visit as the delegate, to bring the nation's condolences. Billy flew directly to Japan to make a phone call to Dr. Bowman, now chairman of the FEBC International Council, and ask for the chairman's help. Billy chose to call from Tokyo, because of possible eavesdropping by the Korean Central Intelligence Agency. They were monitoring Pastor Kim's movements because in the process of setting up the radio station, Billy had gone back and forth to see high-ranking Korean government officials and various politicians. This, coupled with frequent trips to the United States, caused him to be placed on the Korean CIA watch list.

Billy explained his plan to clear the final financial hurdle to the station. "Dr. Bowman, please host a party for Prime Minister Jong Pil Kim while he visits in the United States, and gather all possible politicians from Washington, D.C. Please ask, during that time, for the tax exemption."

Dr. Bowman carried out this plan, and Prime Minister Jong Pil Kim, as soon as he arrived in Korea, instructed the minister of finance to exempt the customs tax for the transmitter.

However, there were further complications. No legal code of law existed exempting a station from the customs tax. Fortunately, Minister Young Sun Kim of the Unification Committee (the committee to seek unification between South and North Korea) purchased the transmitter under the provision of anticommunist broadcasting, and then planned on lending the machine for twenty years to "Asia Broadcasting." This resolved the problem.

However, this unconventional method caused troublesome annual inspections and intervention from the government's Department of Audit. Later, all issues were resolved by having the Asia Broadcasting Company legally assume ownership of the transmitter from the Unification Committee.

NO LONGER IMPOSSIBLE

At last, the Asia broadcast station had been established. On June 30, 1973, officials held a dedication service for the transmitting station. Billy Kim assumed office as the founding director of the Asia Broadcasting Company. It was his first step as the official operator of the business.

If Billy had entertained the thought that the radio station was impossible, it would have surely been impossible. The word "impossible" rises up like a storm when one faces difficulties. Terrifying thoughts take firm root in a person's mind. Truly, the task had seemed impossible. But the moment one says the word "impossible" is when one is captured in the cage of impossibility. A successful worker never considers the word "impossible."

Instead, Billy knew "with God all things are possible" (Matthew 19:26). To a great worker, nothing is impossible with God. Only a little more time is required, perhaps. And maybe a little more effort.

FEBC IN HIS LAP

In the first stage, Asia Broadcasting Company's Seoul office was located in Mukyodong. Later, the office relocated to the third floor of the *Daehan Daily News* building in Taepyungro.

One day Billy sat in the Taepyungro office, fasting in prayer. During those times when the office or ministry faced difficult problems, it was a practice for the entire staff to fast during lunch and pray. This day the staff had received an urgent call from the FEBC headquarters in the United States. It was Dr. Bowman, the chairman.

The Evangelical Alliance Mission (TEAM) had called, suggesting Billy jointly operate TEAM's Far East Broadcasting Company of Korea with the Asia Broadcasting Company. TEAM leaders had called Billy, seeking his opinion as the Asia Broadcasting Company director.

Prior to becoming the director of Asia Broadcast Company, Billy Kim had a close relationship with not only the Far East Broadcasting Company but with TEAM missions. Recall that when Billy had first returned to Korea, it had been a Bob Jones American missionary graduate associated with TEAM who had come with the truck to Incheon to drive their household goods to Suwon. Kim also had many alumni affiliated with TEAM in both the United States and Korea.

Billy even led a program in the Far East Broadcasting Company of Korea, starting in 1962, called "The Youth Hour," personally hosting the program. Moreover, beginning in 1964, he had served the Far East Broadcasting Company of Korea as an executive board member for five years. He had a closer relationship to FEBC than anyone.

On December 23, 1956, Far East Broadcasting Company of Korea had started its first broadcast in Incheon. It had become the third broadcasting company in Korea, after KBS and CBS. It was the second nongovernment private broadcaster in Korean broadcasting history.

FEBC-Korea began suffering extreme financial difficulty in 1970. The debt liability was approximately $600,000, an enormous amount considering Korea's prevailing economic situation.

FEBC-Korea was suffering from more than financial issues. Management was divided because of the so-called Korean denomination, which was undergoing criticism for doctrinal issues. There had been offers from various churches willing to pay 75 percent of their debt, in return for taking over the company. TEAM was clearly aware that the essence of the problem was not only the debt. Therefore, leaders suggested Billy jointly operate FEBC-Korea and the Asia Broadcasting Company, with a view toward more effective missions broadcasting.

Billy prayed with a grieved heart for FEBC-Korea to return to normalcy. As one who managed the Asia Broadcasting Company, he keenly realized how effective a broadcast mission is. He had no reason to hold back.

After much prayer, he soon replied without anguish, "I would gladly accept the proposal of undertaking the joint management of FEBC-Korea." God gave him an extra bonus called FEBC-Korea in his lap. Right away, TEAM sent a welcome to Pastor Billy Kim, trusting that he could effectively handle FEBC-Korea.

Afterward, the FEBC headquarters met with TEAM on several occasions to discuss matters regarding the joint operation of FEBC-Korea. TEAM requested that Billy assume joint management, and in return, FEBC-Korea would pay off all its debt within five years. After the joint management, FEBC-Korea was to be in charge of all its operational costs.

Finally, the two organizations entered into a contract agreement. On January 1, 1977, Pastor Billy Kim became the seventh chairman of FEBC-Korea, with a unanimous vote of approval from the board of directors. In twenty-one years of the Far East Broadcasting Company, it was the very first time that a Korean chairman took office.

WALKING ONE MILE . . . AND MUCH FARTHER

However, he could not take delight in becoming totally responsible for the management. There were many problems that needed to be resolved in order to make it a true missions broadcast. The complete transfer process would take almost two years.

The headquarters of Asia Broadcasting Company had to relocate from the *Daehan Daily News* building in Taepyungro, to the convention building in Sansudong, part of the Mapogu district of Seoul. The Asia Broadcasting Company and Far East Broadcasting Company-Korea had really merged into one.

In 1979, it changed its name from "broadcasting company" to "broadcasting corporation." Billy's title also changed to president. Wilkinson had asked him to go with him a mile. Billy was willing to go two miles, like Jesus had instructed in the Word of God.

Now God was telling Billy to go one hundred, one thousand, and even ten thousand miles on this journey. The Lord made him walk the path of a business manager, something he had never imagined. Billy simply obeyed. The Lord was his Master. He simply took the opportunities God had given.

8

VALUE PEOPLE
AND SAVE MONEY

As Billy Kim took leadership of FEBC-Korea, TEAM presented him a list of people who they believed needed to be fired. Kim looked at the staff list: those recommended for dismissal were underlined in red. Three people even had their name crossed out in red.

However, Billy did not fire anyone. He knew that a diamond-in-the-rough can be found by a good manager. He wanted to give the employees a chance to really show their ability. He understood the heartaches they must have gone through during previous bad management.

The new president believed that the heart of FEBC-Korea operations is the people, those who labor to fulfill the work of the gospel. The Lord called the disciples and directly showed us an example, Kim concluded. Jesus considered His followers precious, as coworkers of the gospel. He thought of them all as "missionaries."

VALUE PEOPLE

Billy Kim also wanted to value people, specifically these employees. Prior to entering the new company, all employees were asked to think of themselves as missionaries in their work. The employees did not let him down. The missionary employees were first to become involved in giving missions offerings and funds to construct a branch broadcasting station in rural areas.

In February 1980, with a goal for economic independence, a "Missions Broadcast $100,000 Fund Campaign" began. The first fund participants were the missionary employees. They all participated in contributing to the fund.

The employees were actively telling the people they met about the necessity of missionary work via radio and the need for funds. They grew in their loyalty to the company as they grew in their self-esteem by being involved in the actual site. The habit of finding difficulties within the company, among the workers' responsibilities, had ended. Each employee/missionary began to take "ownership" of the work.

They understood that they each needed to become a soldier on the front lines of radio missionary work. They also realized that a missions broadcast can only be possible through self-sacrifice, together with the dedication of the listeners of the broadcast.

In his approach to business management, Billy Kim valued people and promoted them according to their abilities, without bias.

For example, FEBC would not operate based on an individual's scholarly background. A graduate of an Ivy League university would not immediately qualify for an important position. Nor would there be any rule that guaranteed their advancement. Advancement within the company was based on ability and dedication to the missionary work rather than educational background or prior experience. In fact, a few head representatives of FEBC branch offices began as company chauffeurs prior to their advancement.

KEY VALUES:
BEING DILIGENT, HUMBLE, AND FRIENDLY

Billy valued how dedicated a person was to the missions broadcast. Each employee must make the work of FEBC their priority above personal matters. They must seek the benefit of FEBC before their own benefit. He valued people who were diligent, humble, and friendly to everyone.

To Billy, valuing people was not limited to staff members. Billy's way was to value people until the end. On one occasion, a dedicated staff member had suddenly passed away, and Billy made certain that his wife would have a position in the FEBC cafeteria, in order to maintain an income for the family. Also, he hired the son to work at FEBC and helped him to attend a nighttime college. That son has now become a college professor.

Once he hired the son of a founding staff member, who later became one of the heads of an FEBC branch office. Occasionally Billy would say, "If any staff member who greatly contributed to the development of the broadcast resigns, and if that person wishes, the company will hire one of the children to continue working here."

In another case, an elderly couple in shabby clothing visited the FEBC-Seoul office one Saturday afternoon. They wanted a tour of FEBC. All the staff had already gone home, and the person on watch duty guided them through the facility and even gave them a cup of hot tea.

Billy had always instructed his staff, "Treat valuably every listener of the broadcast." The elderly couple thanked that staff member for showing them around and handed him an envelope. Before the guide opened the envelope, they said, "We live around the rural outskirts of Kanghwa Island. Actually, we went to visit another gospel broadcasting company this morning but were kicked out by the security guard at the front gate. As we were about to get on the bus back to Kanghwa Island, we felt sadly empty and decided to make a visit to FEBC.

"You have been so kind and friendly in showing us around. In this envelope is something we had prepared to give as an offering to the other broadcast company, but we have decided to offer it instead to FEBC."

Inside was $20,000. It was later discovered that they were an older church couple who owned a gas station near Gimpo. Unknowingly, the FEBC staff person had served an angel couple.

Another story about valuing people came from a recollection of one of the FEBC board of directors, Mr. Kim:

> There was one company that provided prizes for a broadcasting program I was in charge of. One day, the secretary from that company had called. That company was publicly listed on the KOSPI (Korea Composite Stock Price Index) and wanted to give 10 percent of its stock shares as a tithe offering to FEBC. She asked to arrange a meeting with Pastor Billy Kim.
>
> A few days later, Pastor Billy Kim and his secretary, the company CEO and his secretary, and I, the five of us, met together. Pastor Billy Kim then asked, "Why do you want to give it as an offering to FEBC?"
>
> The CEO replied, "I am a church deacon. First and foremost, it is to thank God, and furthermore, I felt that you, Pastor Billy Kim, would use this money wisely for the Lord."
>
> Pastor Billy Kim asked him, "Did you discuss this with your wife, and did she consent to it too?"
>
> The CEO, a little bewildered, replied, "I have not discussed this with my wife yet, but she trusts me, so I am sure she will definitely agree." I was so curious what Pastor Billy Kim's reply would be.
>
> "Just as I wish the best for FEBC, I wish to not cause any trouble in the relationship you have with your wife. Please take it back with you today. After you have discussed the matter with your wife, and if she is delighted to offer it as well, then we will accept it."
>
> I felt knocked on the head with a hammer, shocked and surprised. The money that the CEO was willing to give as an offering was an enormous amount. Ordinarily, even if it was only $10,000, most people would never think twice about accepting it. The CEO is human too and could change his mind in a few days. How could [Billy] be so transcendental in facing such a huge amount of money?
>
> Momentarily, many thoughts rushed through my mind. Ordinarily, I had a lot of respect for Pastor Billy Kim, but witnessing what had just taken place made me fully realize what a big person he was. To Pastor

Kim, people always came before money. The peace and harmony of one family was important above any amount of money. Pastor Billy Kim was someone who truly cared and valued people and their families. What it meant to value people was to give a fair and equal opportunity to the employees that had three red lines crossed over their names.[1]

The incident clearly reveals a business manager who walked step-by-step toward the goal. Such actions encourage individuals to stand up and step forward as well. As a leader, Billy modeled how one must step forward and walk side by side, together, with others. This is treating people without prejudice—not looking at the outer person but seeing each one on the inside.

There's an old saying in Korea, "one ill owner does the work of ten healthy servants." A wise business manager would never want to be the master over the employees.

He would instead make each employee like a master. The employees of FEBC are people who realized their calling as missionaries.

They are managers. They are owners.

SAVE MONEY

At its inception, FEBC stood by three strict principles in its operational management.

First, not a single travel expense was to be given. Second, employee dining expenses should never be used from the broadcasting operation funds. Third, no lobbying would be made to government organizations. The principle was to "use as little as possible, and use only what is absolutely necessary for the spread of the gospel."

In short, the company's goal was "save." This meant not simply save but to save in whatever way and as much as you can—extreme frugality. The employees began calling their boss the "Suwon Miser" or "Suwon Stingy."

Billy wholeheartedly agreed with this criticism. In good humor, he replied, "Yes, I am Suwon Stingy."

Billy said, "People are busy. First, they are busy throwing things away.

They throw away working TVs. They throw away two-hundred-dollar cellphones. They throw away completely fine clothes and shoes, simply because, in today's world, it's out of style. Every self-governing rural province is scrambling to find trash fill sites.

"Things are thrown away, and so new things must be bought. People are busy buying things. In doing so, they need money. People are busy making more money to buy new things.

"People throw away things, and then are busily consumed in living to buy better things.

"Try to save one dollar. Then you are one dollar less busy to make that money.

"You don't need to waste time in throwing it away. You don't have to make the additional dollar. You will find yourself having time to rest, because of that dollar saved."

TREATING GUESTS . . . AND GUESTS TREATING FEBC

Billy Kim tried not to accept lunch or dinner appointments. He would often ask someone to rather give an offering to the broadcast company equal to the cost of food to treat him. There were times, however, when people absolutely insisted on treating him. He was grateful to those people. There were also times when he was required to entertain others—like guests from foreign countries, or people who had provided help, whether big or small, for the company. Billy would make an appointment to treat those people to whom he felt obliged, and then would ask those who insisted on treating him, to join in. This was his way of saving.

The people who wanted to pay to treat Pastor Kim were actually helping FEBC in this way, and those who were being treated felt better, because the money did not come from a pastor with very little income. However, he would never order anything expensive.

Young Hae Kim, Pastor Kim's former secretary and now vice director of Daejun-FEBC, watched his prudent approach to finances: "Pastor Kim would ask me to write the names of all the people who we needed to treat, and then somehow arrange it with the people who wished to treat us. This ultimately saved us money and made the people who were being treated happy as well. He was an expert at this.

"Furthermore, Pastor would prearrange inexpensive, delicious meals that made the person who paid grateful. He frequently told people to spend as little as possible, not to spend it easily, and to be careful in choosing when to spend it," Young Hae recalled. "He asked people to only spend when they had the money. He would ask for offerings only if he was confident that there was sufficient cause to ask."

This was his way of treating a lot of people without using money. Once, Rev. Daniel Lee of Global Mission Church said—with a big smile on his face—"Whenever Pastor Kim asked me to meet at a restaurant, he would always have a sponsor who paid for the meal. Just once, I would like to eat a meal that was paid directly by Pastor Billy Kim."

Normally, when he needed to meet with someone, he would always meet at FEBC. Naturally, he treated people at the FEBC fellowship room, and meals were provided in the FEBC cafeteria. The FEBC fellowship room was always open to anyone. There were all kinds of teas, with fresh baked cookies, at affordable prices. Also the FEBC cafeteria was clean, and the appetizing food was attractively prepared.

Billy did not receive a monthly salary from FEBC, nor any kind of expense fund. When he needed to go on a business trip, most of the travel expense money was returned to the company, because usually the expenses were paid by the invitation host. Even when invited overseas, he normally satisfied his hunger with a simple hamburger. He made it his daily habit not to waste much time on eating or spending excessively on meals.

As one member of the FEBC staff has summarized Billy's approach to food and money, it was to eat simply in order to save money and time. But the staff member added that in saving money one must be ready to spend it without hesitation when it is absolutely necessary for God's kingdom.

FINANCIAL ACCOUNTABILITY

Within FEBC, Billy had set up a unique system called the "Approving Person's Collective Responsibility" (APCR). This was to hold responsible the person who gave approval to a particular business transaction. The system was not implemented as a disciplinary punishment but to place full responsibility on the person making a transaction by requiring that person to repay any money lost from his decision.

Of course, Billy, the final decision maker, was first in line to take most responsibility for any damage compensation required. After him, whoever was next in the line of responsibility would repay their share. It was a heavy price to pay for misusing the offering money that had been given to radio evangelism missionaries.

This is what Rev. Jun Won (David) Kim, branch manager of FEBC–Daejeon Station, has said: "Without Pastor Billy Kim's APCR system, we could well have had lax management of FEBC, resulting in overinvestment in nonproductive areas. This could have caused deterioration of management, or a chronically difficult financial situation. The miraculous growth that we have seen would not have been possible. Once a system was implemented, he made certain that those rules would be carried out."

About twenty years ago a thief came to steal inside the FEBC offices. Every department was robbed of a little, and the president's office was no exception. His secretary should have locked the official funds inside the safe but had forgotten to do so, causing a loss of about two hundred dollars in cash, which she had left on top of the desk.

After hearing this, Billy personally paid back one hundred dollars, being responsible for having a forgetful secretary, and the remaining one hundred dollars was to be paid back by the secretary, as part of her responsibility. He clearly asked others to be responsible for their mistakes, but he first took his own responsibility, which was Billy's way of giving a personal reprimand.

GAIN MUCH FROM LITTLE

Saving money does not simply mean to conserve or to be frugal. One principle was to gain the greatest possible result from minimal expenditure, and another was to always be prepared to overcome any unforeseen crisis expense. Billy's secret method for gaining the greatest result from minimal expenditure is illustrated by gift baskets, Secretaries Meetings, and broadcast environment changes.

In Korean culture, companies and individuals alike are required to give gifts to personal or business associates on major holidays. At these times, FEBC staff would be busy making and delivering egg baskets at Easter, Korean rice cake baskets during Thanksgiving, and cookie baskets for Christmas. Personally delivering these baskets demonstrated heartfelt gratitude toward the dedicated people who had helped FEBC.

Instead of plain floral baskets, they were filled with eggs, rice cakes, cookies, fruit, beverages, candies, biscuits, etc., which looked quite pleasing to the eye, yet not costly. It had become a popular seasonal basket that people anticipated as each season arrived. Even though it was a small basket, it demonstrated that FEBC remembered and appreciated their prayers and support.

Ever since 1982, the annually held Secretaries Meeting was another highly effective event, which was possible with a nominal expense. The Secretaries Meeting was a festival for the secretaries of many companies and organizations that had helped FEBC. They were invited to a dinner, while they watched performances and shared time with each other. Billy understood the difficulties that secretaries face. He understood how much of a difference they made. Those attending the meeting had been glad to assist with anything relating to FEBC, and this was the reason for the event.

BE PREPARED FOR A CRISIS EXPENSE

Another principle was to always be prepared to overcome any unforeseen crisis expense. Ongoing cost savings was the key way to prepare for the unexpected expenses during a crisis. When the International Monetary Fund crisis struck Korea in 1997, FEBC-Korea's cost-saving approach proved extremely effective. Other broadcasting companies underwent intense hardships in trying to manage the high cost of production, but FEBC did not suffer financially throughout the turmoil of the IMF crisis.

ADOPTING NEW TECHNOLOGY

FEBC also was an early adopter of new methods to lower their costs. A good example of a low-cost method for systems operation was the

"Ana-Duo System." The Ana-Duo System is a radio program production system that combines in one person the role of three people—an announcer, a producer, and an operator. FEBC was the first Korean radio broadcasting company to introduce this Ana-Duo System. In the beginning, there were quite a few employees who opposed the idea.

In the United States there were so many small local radio stations that this method had become a generally accepted idea. However, Korea had only a few national broadcasting companies, and in Korea this new technology represented an unprecedented approach. Other broadcasters in the area did not understand the concept and scoffed at FEBC, considering the broadcaster as practicing at an amateur level.

In the beginning, there were many operational mistakes. However, as time passed, FEBC staff became skilled, multitasking operators, who understood all that went into the production of a program. Even the quality of the programs improved greatly, and the operational expenses declined significantly.

Other broadcast companies soon became interested in FEBC's Ana-Duo System and visited FEBC to observe and study it. Now, many broadcasters in Korea seek overall efficiency through the Ana-Duo System.

One broadcast company indicated in its advertising that they were looking for someone capable of handling the Ana-Duo System, and that they preferred workers who had experience with FEBC. One business manager's amazing foresight into a possible future crisis, and his determination to bring in new methods, brought a noteworthy change to the Korean radio broadcasting industry.

BENEFITS OF BROADCASTING AUTOMATION

Billy also implemented broadcasting automation in the early 1990s to keep in step with other changes occurring in the broadcast industry. APC (Automatic Program Control) brought in the latest technological equipment with computer systems, to reach the goal of acquiring a higher level of efficiency in production. Automation means that the machines free people to spend more time producing higher quality programs, as well as being more economically efficient. Automation maximizes the efficiency of a radio broadcast and is the shortest path to low-cost management.

Not surprisingly, implementation of automated systems caused a few staff officers to raise their hands in disapproval. Nevertheless, Billy aggressively carried forward implementation with his own unique driving force. As a result, the automated systems proved to be successful in many ways.

Nighttime broadcasting benefited greatly from these labor savings. These broadcasts had required staff members to take turns staying up every night, to ensure that the broadcast was properly transmitted. Now one staff person could operate the station during the overnight hours. If such systems had not been implemented, the current branch broadcasting stations would not have been possible.

PERSONAL VERSUS OFFICIAL MONEY

Another principle that Pastor Kim established regarding money was to clearly distinguish between "personal" and "official" money. When he was invited to appear for outside events, he sometimes received money envelopes as a gesture of gratitude. This could be a guest speaker's pay or simply a personal gift. Billy usually did not know how much money the envelopes contained. Most of the time, he did not open the envelope but gave it to the staff person who had accompanied him. The accompanying staff person immediately deposited the money with the accounts department. Afterward FEBC sent an acknowledgment receipt, with a thank-you letter from Pastor Billy Kim.

Most of this money had been given as an expression of gratitude toward him. Was this a gift of money that could have been considered "personal" money? His reply was, "That is absolutely not the case. That money rightfully belongs to FEBC.

"I had not been invited there as 'Billy Kim, the person.' I was invited there as 'FEBC president, Billy Kim.' Therefore, I received that money through FEBC. It is therefore company funds. I most definitely cannot keep that money."

The overarching principle applied to the FEBC staff as well. If one felt even a little hesitant about keeping any given money, most probably it was because it's a public fund. FEBC policy required that one strictly distinguish between public and private funds. Unless absolutely differentiated, it confuses one's mind to think of it as your own money. Had Kim not been abundantly clear about this, there could have been many offerings that would simply be missing, unknown, and unacknowledged. Instead, everyone who ever gave to FEBC knew right away that their offering had been received; FEBC would immediately send them a receipt. The giver would realize how honestly it was deposited, and how honestly it would be used.

Similarly, one must never open an envelope before giving it to their accounting staff to see how the money is designated. Our Lord gives great abundance of money only to the honest steward.

Finally, even when faced with the financial struggles and debts of FEBC, Billy still gave a tithe with a strict distinction to other missionary organizations. This clearly demonstrates how he had lived as a good steward. Being called as a good steward not only means diligently gathering and saving. It also means diligently sharing. Perhaps that is why God had entrusted him with five talents.

9

MANAGE IN THE
LORD'S WAY

B illy had the financial independence of FEBC-Korea in his mind from the time of his inauguration as FEBC-Korea president. The first place he made cuts was on the board of directors. Some of the board directors had been using travel expenses from FEBC-Korea accounts for various reasons. This practice did not seem to fit with the task of radio missionary work. The members of the board who used transportation expenses were replaced with those who willingly gave toward missions offerings. There was opposition from existing board members, but his stand was firm.

Billy worked personally without being paid a salary and not using travel expenses. He traveled in and out of the country, raising funds for the company. He incorporated wonderful elders in the faith into the board of directors, who could truly help FEBC. From the beginning of his management, Billy tried hard to promote the concept that FEBC is a mission field where one pays and works. It was a work philosophy that cannot be understood in the world's concept of management, yet from the perspective of the gospel, it is justifiably correct.

COMING UP SHORT

TEAM consistently paid down FEBC-Korea's past debt, as had been promised. However, gaining financial independence was not an easy task. On the day the two broadcasting companies actually merged (June 30, 1978), it rained heavily during the morning hours. The secretary was busy placing metal buckets here and there to catch the rain leaking in the office. Billy quietly sat on his chair, steadily gazing at those metal buckets. One of the metal buckets had a crack in the bottom of it. The water had leaked through the crack, spilling entirely on the floor. There was no way the buckets would be filled with those few drops of rain.

He fell into deep thought. "It's like the broadcasting company's bank balance." Since the early morning hours, his nerves had been on edge as he looked at the documents that required his approval. That day was the employees' payday. Scraping to the last penny, he was still short about five thousand dollars. Even if he approved the transaction, there was no way that the full amount could be given. He was in a position to personally loan the money to meet the payroll. However, in FEBC-Korea's current debt situation, the bank would not approve of him doing so.

He envisioned the faces of the employees one by one, including the faces of his own family, whom he hardly had time to see. On paydays, monthly rents along with electricity bills were due. Things like a sack of rice and the doctor's fee for a mother were needed. Children's tuitions were due. For the past thirty days, everyone had waited for that much needed payday.

Billy Kim felt like an incompetent CEO, who couldn't pay for even the small salaries, after requiring employees to work from the break of dawn to late at night. His heart ached.

Of course he could say a lot about how the company's financial situation had come about. He wanted to shout how hard he had worked to raise funds, day and night until his feet blistered, without receiving even a dime as his own paycheck. He thought of petitioning everyone to join in suffering for the purpose of spreading the gospel. However, he remained silent. He personally carried the responsibility as the CEO.

Whatever excuses or divine reasons he could think of, he could not avoid criticisms as a CEO who could not pay salaries. No matter what he did, the bank account balance would not increase.

Suddenly, he felt a lump of sorrow rise in his throat. He wept unrestrainedly. He fell prostrate on the floor. The wet and heavy scent of the floor irritated his nostrils. He tried praying without success. For a good while, he just vented in tears. How long had he cried?

THE LORD'S MANAGEMENT

The telephone rang. It was the secretary. Elder Kyung Sub Lim had come to visit and was waiting outside. He was a rear admiral of the navy who had been transferred to the first reserve list. Billy had met him on several occasions in regard to the withdrawal of the American military forces in Korea, when Elder Lim had been the head of the Korean Naval Intelligence Advisory Board. He quickly wiped away his tears and went out to greet him.

"Pastor, I have come to help in the broadcast missions through FEBC, but . . . it seems your eyes are swollen." After hearing that he had come, wanting to help in the broadcast missions, Billy openly shared his heartaches, which had tormented his mind since that morning. Elder Lim responded with a moved expression on his face and left, promising that he would return shortly.

Two hours later, Elder Lim called back. "Pastor, it's done!" His voice seemed excited with joy. Elder Lim, as soon as he had left the office, called his fellow in faith, Elder Myeong Bok Lee, and explained to him about the financial state of FEBC-Korea. He told Elder Lee that he wanted to lend around five thousand dollars. But Elder Lee said that he wanted to donate the entire amount as an offering, rather than lending it.

Billy repeatedly thanked him and hung up.

Immediately, he fell on his knees before God. He confessed his sin in thinking even for a short while that it was "his" company. He repented of his mistake of acting like a master and not like a servant. He admitted his incompetence by only worrying and not doing anything about it. While he had sat in a daze on his chair viewing the company's insufficient balance like the cracked metal bucket, the Lord was ceaselessly working. The actual one giving the salary to the employees was the "True Manager of FEBC"—our Lord God. Billy declared in a loud voice, "Lord, You are the true CEO of FEBC!"

His Lord's management support did not end with just that one time. Thereafter, Elder Kyeong Sub Lim promised along with Elder Myeong Bok Lee, Elder Jin Woo Lee, and Elder Hang Su Lee to give an offering toward a portion of the insufficient amount of the employees' monthly salary. The four elders' promise was not individual people acting, Billy realized, but the active provision of God on the firm rock of faith.

This promise was the beginning of the FEBC-Korea Steering Committee. This committee, which was formed by the promise of God, grew to seventy members within one year and continues to be one of the most important groups of supporters.

In 1980, the Korean press and media industry underwent a whirlwind of consolidation and reorganization. Many broadcasting and newspaper companies had to close due to the consolidation, resulting in the layoff of numerous journalists and reporters. Every time he heard news about restructuring, Billy's heart fell. Next could be FEBC-Korea.

It was a nerve-wracking time for all of radio. But FEBC leaders soon learned that FEBC-Korea would be exempt from government mandates of restructuring, because it did not broadcast any news and aired very little Korean language programming.

The Lord had kept FEBC-Korea safe from the sharp blades that had carved through the media industry at that time.

As FEBC overcame the difficulty of government intervention, and the restructuring of broadcasting companies, Billy Kim set his mind to free the company from any leasing obligations. Yet he wondered how that could be possible when he still had a hard time paying the employees. Still, he wanted to build a church to God, for the purpose of spreading the gospel through broadcast missions. He did not want the Lord's precious gospel to be in a constant state of uncertainty.

BUILDING A CHURCH FOR BROADCAST MISSIONS

In order to acquire a mission base building, Billy reasoned the best way was to purchase land with an existing building, then rebuild or expand the structure. He soon looked toward the Compassion Building, registered under the name "Swanson Memorial Foundation."

Pastor Swanson, while serving as the chaplain for the US military during the Korean War, had begun an evangelistic organization to help orphans. Eventually he was called the father of war orphans. The organization purposed to focus on spiritual salvation, along with other missionary work.

He passed away in 1965, and the following year, to commemorate his life, the Swanson evangelistic organization's Compassion Building was built.

Billy met with the Swanson Foundation preservation board, and expressed his wish for them to give the Compassion Building[1] as an offering and to dedicate it for the FEBC-Korea main headquarters. FEBC now leased part of the building. The preservation board responded very positively. However, the government opposed the donation. Due to the characteristics of a foundation, registration cannot be transferred to a different type of organization. According to the government, the Compassion Building Foundation was registered under the Department of Social Welfare, whereas FEBC-Korea was registered under the Department of Culture & Information. Any purchase transactions or registration transfer was absolutely impossible. The government administration's position was firm.

However, Billy still wanted to purchase the Compassion Building for the FEBC-Korea headquarters. Every morning and night, he prayed for this to be possible. He visited the various government departments regularly. He was persistent. Pastor Swanson's purpose in coming to Korea was to share the good news of the gospel with the many war-stricken, suffering people. FEBC's purpose was to share the good news of the gospel with the many people under communism, who were deprived of their right to religious freedom, he argued. The purpose was really the same. There was no difference.

"If Pastor Swanson was alive, he would surely have given it for this purpose," Billy said. The most honorable way to commemorate Pastor Swanson would be to follow his purpose in life to spread the gospel. It was an act of obedience to God's command, to be witnesses "to the end of the earth" (Acts 1:8).

Regardless of whether the government administration officials were listening or not, he continued to call on them to make this possible. "The foundational purpose of the Compassion Building is the same as that of FEBC!" he told any who would listen.

God did not look away from his prayers and efforts at persuasion. FEBC-Korea finally did receive legal permits from the government to transfer the ownership of the Compassion Building as well as the land. To God, nothing is impossible.

Pastor Swanson's commemorative building was located in the Kwonsundong district of Suwon. Billy used his personal money to purchase the land, as an offering for the new Pastor Swanson commemorative site. He believed it was a small amount to pay in comparison to what the broadcasting mission would gain in return. He knew the gain was not for himself but for God, and Billy was very happy.

After gaining ownership of the Compassion Building, the conditions were not different from when they were leasing it. This structure also had rainwater slipping through ceilings. The small amount of space had not changed either.

Repair and expansion would require a large sum of money, about $100,000. In order to make this happen, he decided to "run for it"—even if his shoes wore out in the process. Everywhere he spoke, every individual he met, he would emphasize the importance of a missions broadcast. Even if someone offered $100, Billy ran for it from dawn until late at night, regardless of the distance.

During those days, Pastor Billy Kim had a solid reputation; less than ten years had passed since his duties translating at the Billy Graham Crusade in Seoul, and he continued to be invited as a main speaker, both in and outside the country. This now famous national pastor would run to any small church willing to offer even one hundred dollars. This may have seemed strange—not only to the public but also to the FEBC-Korea staff.

A PASSIONATE YET HUMBLE FUNDRAISER

Billy always stood facing God as "Billy the houseboy," "Jang Hwan Kim, a servant of God."

Picking up the mantle from college friend David Wilkinson, Billy Kim catches the vision for Christian radio into China, Russia, and North Korea. FEBC President Kim has an office in the 1984 FEBC headquarters in Seoul. A new building opens in 2013.

FEBC-Jeju, close to China, would be the first broadcast station Kim would establish (1973). Later a more powerful series of antennae were dedicated to extend the broadcast signal. FEBC–Bangsan (right) soon reached into North Korea.

FEBC-Mokpo headquarters (top); FEBC-Busan, 93.3 FM, broadcasts a special thanksgiving service to celebrate its second anniversary in 2010.

Trudy Kim celebrates a student birthday during class. During graduation at Central Kindergarten, she presents a Bible to one of her students.

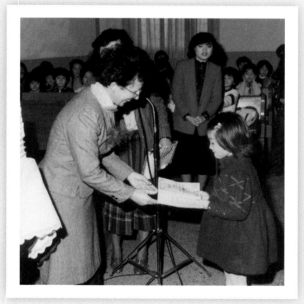

Students board bus to Central Kindergarten and then celebrate their arrival. Trudy was the first teacher and later superintendent of Central Kindergarten. She receives a bouquet of flowers at the dedication of Central Christian Academy.

Central Christian Academy, serving students from kindergarten to grade ten, has been commended for its modern design. The Christian Center (bottom) has been used by the academy, the Suwon Christian Church, and Suwon Youth for Christ.

Billy Kim holds door open for First Lady Yook Young Soo, who arrives for the dedication of Suwon Christian Hospital. Pastor Kim founded the hospital as well as Suwon Central Elder Care Home and helped to found Youth for Christ in Korea.

Teens respond to the invitation to receive Christ as Savior at Youth For Christ meeting. For his service to the youth and elderly, and bringing spiritual comfort to those in Korea and abroad through FEBC radio, Dr. Billy Kim received the Mugunghwa Medal, the Order of Civil Merit, the highest decoration given to a Korean citizen.

He always endeavored to remain humble. He considered the magnitude of God's gospel and chose to become nothing. He was content if his fame would be like a cane, leading him to further spread the gospel. People became fond of his passion and of his humility.

Passion can lead to pride. Humility can sometimes be viewed as incompetence. Billy remained passionate yet humble. His attitude made many open their hearts. Many voluntarily opened their wallets as well. This was how he was able to raise funds. His passion, led by humility, had raised the needed $100,000.

He could not sleep for days in the excitement of knowing an additional floor would not only provide the much needed space but also fix the leaking roof as well. However, the dream turned to ashes when he was told by building safety inspectors that due to the poor condition of the building, an additional floor would be impossible. The disappointment Billy and all the staff felt was beyond words.

Elder Kyung Sub Lee, who was vice president, suggested, "Let's tear down the original building and construct a new one." There was no other option. After days of anguish, the cost of rebuilding was referred to a professional for appraisal. Two million dollars were needed. They concluded that it would be impossible. Instead, a separate structure would be built on the vacant part of the land. The design was to have three stories above and one floor below ground level, on approximately 10,676 square feet (one quarter acre) of land. It consisted of various studio rooms and an open hall. This would cost $600,000.

Leaders calculated another full five years would be needed to raise these funds. If possible, FEBC President Kim wanted to broadcast the gospel to believers inside communist nations much sooner.

GOD'S CONSTRUCTION PLAN

In the middle of all the calculations and dream, Billy received an urgent call to come to the hospital. In Deuk Kim, Chairman of Byucksan Co., who was on the board of directors, explained that his wife, Deaconess Hyun Eui Yoon,[2] was hospitalized with cancer. It was worsening.

"Pastor, my time has come to go to my Lord," she said when he stood by her bed. She was clearly aware of her imminent death. Nevertheless, Deaconess Yoon's face was more at peace than at any other time. "I have one thing I'll miss. I'll miss having a part in the missions broadcast to the communist nations. This has always been in my heart." She was passionate for the gospel broadcast like no one else, while she had been healthy. She had been a faithful gospel evangelist.

"Please, you must get well soon. When you recover your health, you can continue to be a part of spreading the gospel to communist nations." Billy held Deaconess Yoon's hand and earnestly prayed. He truly prayed that she would get up straightaway.

"I've been praying for the missionary work to the communist nations. It would be so good if I could regain health . . . and I would be so happy if I could see the day when I would again be a part of the sharing of the gospel." She paused, and tears welled up in her eyes. "Even if I can't, I want to leave something special for this purpose."

Not many days after his visit, Deaconess Yoon was called to the Lord. Her words of wanting to "leave something special for evangelizing the communist nations" became clear in her final will. Mr. Kim gave an offering of $500,000 according to his wife's will. He was on the FEBC-Korea board of directors, and knew so well how fully dedicated FEBC-Korea was in spreading the gospel to communist countries. Of course, he also knew well that the mission broadcast was in great need of the $500,000.

On August 17, 1984, through the precious offering of In Deuk Kim's wife, a separate FEBC-Korea complex was completed. In remembrance of Deaconess Hyun Eui Yoon's wishes to spread the gospel to communist nations, the new building was named "Hyun Eui Memorial."

However, God's construction plan did not end there. The Holy Spirit moved on the heart of another man, Elder Soon Young Choi of the Shindongah Group, who was also on the FEBC-Korea board of directors. Elder Choi's hidden help behind the scenes had a great impact on FEBC-Korea to develop into what it is today. Billy was deeply grateful to Elder Choi for all the cooperation he had given. Now Elder Choi announced that he would demolish the original, run-down Compassion Building and completely build the new four-story FEBC-Korea main headquarters, free of charge.

What Billy and all the staff had thought "impossible" had suddenly become "possible" with God.

Everyone was convinced the missions broadcasting "temple"—FEBC-Korea, the main headquarters office—was planned, drafted, and constructed by God Himself. In September 1986, the Lord had provided the main headquarters office building for FEBC-Korea. It was the time for dedicating a "temple" for the spreading of the gospel through sound waves, for evangelizing North Korea and other nearby regions.

It had been exactly nine years since Billy took office at FEBC-Korea.

MARCHING TOWARD
A BIGGER DREAM

The dreams of FEBC had been to have its message reach beyond Korea to communist lands nearby—China, Russia, and yes, North Korea, once part of a united Korea. The biggest dream was, of course, North Korea, where friends and even families lived. There would be many steps along the way to accomplishing those dreams.

Increasing the signal strength of existing radio stations would help. In 1987, a project began to double the 50,000-watt signal of the Seoul station. Raising the signal strength to 100,000 watts was necessary in order to transmit with better clarity to wider regions of the communist nations. However, two problems had to be solved before a more powerful signal could be realized.

First, both from Korea domestically and the International Telecommunication Union (ITU), FEBC-Korea had to obtain permissions from Korea's neighboring countries of China, Japan, and North Korea—all gospel-disliking nations. It was clear that they would not likely agree to allow the increase in broadcasting power.

Second, a higher-frequency transmitter would require $480,000. Considering FEBC-Korea's bank balance, this was a huge cost.

A STEP CLOSER TO THE NORTH

Both problems would be difficult to overcome. But Billy Kim began the work, both through prayer and personal energy. The greater signal would allow the station to take a giant step to the north.

In order to visit the ITU Convention, Billy had to go to Geneva, Switzerland. On July 16, 1986, Myeong Ku Lee, director of the FEBC engineering department, joined him on the journey. "This visit might just be in vain, so please don't expect too great an outcome," Lee cautioned. He knew very well how difficult a task it was, and out of concern that Billy would be very disappointed from the cold response from ITU, Lee warned him of what might be the outcome.

Even during the FEBC-Korea staff meeting, almost everyone had concluded that increasing the power signal was impossible. Dr. Kim, now having worked in the broadcasting field for approximately ten years, also knew how difficult this task would be.[1] He himself did not expect a great outcome from this initial visit. Nevertheless, he had faith that it would be done, knowing well that God had been leading in this matter.

The Lord already had others working there to aid in the process. The key person in charge at the convention was, surprisingly, a Korean. It was Ki Su Lee, himself a faithful church elder. Billy and his accompanying staff were overwhelmed with joy in seeing him. There was not even a single cold response. On the contrary, Mr. Lee warmly grabbed hold of Billy's hands with both of his, saying, "You came all the way here, just for the purpose of evangelizing the northern regions?" God had already been working through Mr. Lee.

Kim and engineering director Myeong Ku Lee rejoiced when they eventually heard they would receive permission to increase the wattage of their radio station. After this, FEBC-Korea would face many opposing appeals from the neighboring countries. However, Elder Ki Su Lee continually took on the key role of being the shield of protection. The following year, in August, the National Telecommunications Administration Bureau (NTAB) gave its final approval.

Even the fundraising, which had begun prior to the request to raise the signal strength, had gone smoothly. Many regular listeners participated. Among them, a blind brother in the Lord donated $3,000, and this pricked the hearts of others. He was only a masseur. He had given his hard-earned cash, which he had saved, little by little, sweating and massaging until his arms ached. Billy mentioned to others that the masseur was a greater broadcasting evangelist than he was.

Finally, on June 12, 1988, the transmitter relocated from Incheon to Bangsan, not far from the provincial capital of Seoul and just thirty-three miles (via direct radio signals) to Kaesong, the nearest North Korea city, and with 100,000 watts, the signal went much farther north. FEBC had realized their dream of bringing the gospel deep into Korea's northern communist state; the signal also reached into parts of China and Russia.

EXPANDING INTO RUSSIA

God wanted the FEBC broadcasts to reach even farther into the northern regions. In October of 1991, during the FEBC conference held in England, Billy proposed the establishing of FEBC-Russia. Although Russian programming crossed into international boundaries through the Bangsan transmitter, a station closer to the Russian border would permit even greater penetration of the gospel. Those attending agreed on the suggestion and resolved to establish an FEBC-Russia at the Khabarovsk area, near China's Heilongjiang province. There, tens of thousands of North Koreans worked in lumberyards.

The following year, beginning on March 15, once a day for one hour, broadcasts in English and Korean were aired.

At first, FEBC leased the Khabarovsk's broadcast network—POR-8. However, this was temporary. For a regular broadcast to take place, an FEBC-Khabarovsk headquarters had to be established. FEBC-Korea took charge of the new construction.

Again, prayers and fundraising began. This time, the fundraising miracles came from the FEBC-Korea Women's Operation Committee. The

Women's Operation Committee hosted a bazaar to raise $30,000 but the actual event raised three times more, netting $100,000! Even after the event, many broadcasting missionaries contributed to the fund.

On June 1, 1995, FEBC-Korea opened their doors in the heart of the formerly communist nation of Russia. The FEBC-Khabarovsk headquarters aired the gospel of Christ, twenty-four hours a day. God made it possible for all the FEBC transmitting towers to stand—for the sole purpose of spreading the gospel to the northern regions. To the broadcasters, those transmitting towers, raised high above the ground, became reminders of the cross of love that Christ bore for all. Through them, the Holy Spirit–anointed, lifesaving message of the gospel was poured down every minute, like the early and late rain, upon desperately needy people to quench their thirst.

STATIONS ACROSS THE KOREAN PENINSULA

God not only presided over FEBC to reach the northern regions but also to every corner of the Korean peninsula. Billy planned to establish FEBC regional branch offices. The first one was in Daejeon. FEBC-Daejeon opened its temporary branch office in 1989. On April 10, after the dedication worship service, the first branch office officially hung up their signboard and began office work.

On July 3, the legal permit was granted for the broadcast, and on December 1 at four o'clock in the afternoon, the first radio transmission was launched. This began a new chapter called the FEBC Regional Broadcast.

By its fifth anniversary, FEBC-Daejeon had its own office building comprised of a basement and three stories above ground. This had been made possible through a 660-pyeong (about one-half acre) lot donated by a Daejeon Christian businessman.

The future FEBC-Changwon would endure many ups and downs prior to its establishment. In 1992, the official permit request was flatly denied. For three long years the regional Christian believers continued to pray together and campaign for its permit. Nevertheless, the permits did not come easily.

Christians gathered from the regions of Masan and Changwon and planned to hold a large rally at the Masan Indoor Stadium for the establishment of FEBC-Changwon. Non-Christians typically viewed the planned rally as a protest, but to the believers it was simply a dedicated prayer gathering.

Nevertheless, the rally was not held—because it was no longer necessary. Just prior to the rally date, in May 1995, FEBC-Changwon had dramatically obtained its permit. The many prayers prior to the planned prayer rally had been heard; less than two years later (March 16, 1997), FEBC-Changwon was established. Soon afterward, naturally, fundraising began for the construction of its office building, and FEBC-Changwon dedicated its base building in November of 1999.

The drive to establish FEBC-Mokpo began when the chief executive officer of the Shinwon Group Co., Ltd., provided the office on the second floor of Jeonnam Laity Seminary. The board of directors approved the location as well as the setup plan of the Asia Broadcasting headquarters in Honam. Two years later the Honam headquarters office, along with its studios, were relocated in the city of Mokpo.

FEBC-Mokpo broadcast its first radio programs on April 2, 2001, into the Jeonnam (the most southern parts of the Korean peninsula Jeollanam-do) and the Seonnam regions (the most southwest part of Korea). Meanwhile, a permit was issued for FEBC-Sokcho in January of 1999, which aired its first trial broadcast on December 1 of that year.

In establishing these regional FEBC branch offices to cover all areas of limited reception within Korea, funding was greatly lacking. Billy had close ties with the US DeMoss Foundation, which offered $670,000 in a "Matching Fund" contribution. In order to receive the full $670,000 from the DeMoss Foundation, Billy had to first raise the equivalent amount.

MOVING A SIGNAL CLOSER TO NORTH KOREA

In May 2001, FEBC-Sokcho changed its official name to FEBC-Yeongdong, and its transmitting tower was relocated to Mt. Kwebang, the best possible location for clearer reception in the North Korean regions—near the North Korean border and the Mt. Keumkang tourist region. The shape of Korea's eastern seacoast made it possible to hear the transmission in North Korea with ease. Meanwhile, FEBC Bangsan/Seoul continued to broadcast into western North Korea.

In recent years, as more bilateral economic exchanges occurred between South and North Korea, South Korean workers who had been sent to North Korea's Najin Sunbong region returned with reports that they were able to hear the broadcasts from FEBC-Yeongdong very clearly.

The Asia Broadcasting-Jeju station had grown to become the Jeju headquarters in 1993, airing its own programs and having its own broadcast schedule from Jeju Island. The following year, it was able to complete its headquarters building, funded primarily by the Christian believers from Jeju Island and Honam, on the southern end of the Korean peninsula. In October of 2001, as Asia Broadcasting and FEBC-Korea merged, the official name changed to FEBC-Jeju.

FEBC-KOREA NETWORK

SEOUL
극동방송(중앙사)
1188kHz (AM)
106.9MHz (FM)

YEONGDONG
영동극동방송
90.1MHz
102.9MHz
100.9MHz

LOS ANGELES
LA극동방송
1230kHz

DAEJEON
대전극동방송
93.3MHz

IKSAN
익산
91.1MHz

DAEGU
대구극동방송
91.9MHz

POHANG
포항극동방송
90.3MHz

ULSAN
울산극동방송
107.3MHz

GWANGJU
광주극동방송
93.1MHz

CHANGWON
창원극동방송
98.1MHz

BUSAN
부산극동방송
93.3MHz

MOKPO
목포극동방송
100.5MHz

JEJU
제주극동방송
1566kHz (AM)
101.1MHz (FM / 서귀포)

RECENT EXPANSION AND RECOGNITION

Today, as a Korean private broadcaster, FEBC-Korea transmits with their greatest frequency ever of 250 kw, shooting up to thirty miles into the stratosphere, which is reflected back to be heard even in the distant regions of Kazakhstan, 2,800 miles away. FEBC-Korea now broadcasts the truth of the gospel to a 1.7 billion population of the northeast Asian regions of Korea, China, Japan, and Russia.

Other stations soon began in Pohang, Ulsan, and Kyeongnam. FEBC-Pohang began its operation on November 12, 2001. On the fourth anniversary of its founding, in March 2005, FEBC-Pohang relocated its office to a new building in Duksandong. This station is broadcasting to the areas of Pohang, Kyeongju, Yeongchun, Yeongduk, etc., airing the truth of the gospel twenty-four hours a day to 1.3 million souls.

The cities of Ulsan and Kyeongnam, on the farthest southeast regions of the Korean peninsula, heard FEBC-Ulsan's first broadcast on February 25, 2002. The station reached 4.5 million people with the truth of the gospel. Shortly after its fifth anniversary, FEBC-Ulsan relocated its office to their new building in Daldong, of Namgu.

The Busan studio base began its foundational setup plans in December 2001, when FEBC-Changwon was established. For a long period Busan, on its own, had to go through the process of collecting signatures and raising funds. Finally, on April 26, 2008, FEBC-Busan was established. On the station's second anniversary, supporters dedicated FEBC-Busan's own new building by hosting a special worship service. All who attended were moved, with thankful hearts for what God had done. Two years later permit approval came for a station in Daegu, and on January 10, 2011, FEBC-Daegu began broadcasting.

During all this growth, the broadcasting corporation was being recognized for its contributions to the country. In 1982, the Korean government presented Billy Kim with the Order of Merit, the Dongbaek Medal. In 1992 he was awarded the highest decoration of the Civil Merit, the Mugunghwa Medal, for his contributions to exchange relations with the northern regions. In addition, the National Religious Broadcasters, in 2006, presented Billy the Individual Achievement in International Broadcasting Award.

Nevertheless, Billy emphasized, "What I receive as an award or a medal in the world is only because I represent FEBC-Korea, but my true personal award is prepared in the heavenly kingdom."

A HIDDEN STASH OF CASH

Billy clearly remembered an incident a dozen years earlier. In May 1993, an urgent call had come from an Incheon port official who had detained an ethnic Korean Chinese woman. They had scanned her and had discovered that she had hidden a large sum of US money in her clothing. She was constantly asking for Pastor Jang Hwan Kim, of FEBC-Korea. He postponed an appointment with an important guest and headed straight toward Incheon harbor with another staff member from FEBC-Korea.

Together with six other ethnic Korean Chinese believers, the woman worshiped with a secret church and listened to the FEBC-Korea broadcast in her region of communist China. They kept their faith without a single Bible or a single hymnal for twenty-two years, by listening to the broadcast and growing in their faith. FEBC-Korea was their Bible, hymnal, and church. And now she wanted to speak with Pastor Kim.

After Billy and an assistant arrived, she relayed her story to them and the port official. One day, through prayer, one of their members decided they should give FEBC-Korea a thank offering for blessing them with the gospel of God's grace. That person had suggested during their six-member gathering, "How beautiful and great are the blessings we have received until now! Let us not use a single penny from the allowances sent to us from our children, and let us give it all to God."

They had all agreed to this with one heart and prepared a jar. Every time they gathered to worship, they put into the jar the money sent from their children, and whatever they could give from selling goods, saving bus fares by walking instead for an hour and a half, and money saved by not buying goodies for their grandchildren, etc. Each time, they sealed the lid with candle wax because it was their offering to God, which meant they could not use it for any other purpose. It was also necessary to prevent any loss or theft.

However, as time passed, rumors began to circulate that these elders had a lot of cash. Finally, one of the members, after discussing it with the others, concluded by saying, "Let's send this offering to FEBC-Korea, which has been our church." After careful consideration as to who to send to deliver the offering, they selected the youngest person among them, a thirty-three-year old unmarried woman, Myung Ja Choi (a pseudonym). They had resolved this, thinking that she would be less burdened than the others, since she was not yet married. The money the port authority discovered was the gift they had hoped to give to Kim.

"Myung Ja! Please come back after delivering this offering to Pastor Jang Hwan Kim of the FEBC-Korea," the elders said.

"Me? Why should I be the one?" In a communist nation, smuggling foreign currency was like a death sentence. Miss Choi fasted for two days in prayer before deciding. Afterward, she purposed to obey her belief that it was God's will.

"I shall go and return. If I get caught by security police on my way there, I will jump into the sea and drown myself." She prepared to leave, determined even to face death. Inside the outer coat, US money was evenly distributed. Another layer of fabric was placed and stitched, like in a padded quilted jacket, avoiding the areas where the cash was hidden. To be safer, she took a boat instead of a plane. They thought that the security search would be less stringent on the boat.

The moment after Miss Choi started on the journey, other members of the church started relay prayers. They awoke daily at one o'clock in the morning, secretly worshiping God in prayer, after which they slept for a few hours. Then, they got up at the break of dawn and went to the mountains to collect mountain herbs, balloon flower roots, and wild edible greens, etc., which they dried and sold at the markets, along with pickled radish. They lived impoverished lives, selling only those few things. They had to work and took turns every day in prayers. One person would pray while the others went to the mountains. Then another person would come, after working in the mountains, to take the baton in prayer, in a continual relay.

They asked Miss Choi, prior to departure, "If you succeed in delivering this, please ask Pastor Jang Hwan Kim to tell us through the radio broadcast, on a certain date in May, at what time and minute he received it. Until we hear his voice of confirmation through the broadcast, we will continually pray and wait for it."

Miss Choi had arrived safely in two days at the Port of Incheon. However, the dollars she had hidden showed up on the X-ray scanner. Without giving any explanation for such a large amount of cash, the woman from China, in awkward attire, repeatedly asked the security guard for Pastor Jang Hwan Kim. Finally, the security guard contacted Billy.

When Billy arrived to meet with Miss Choi, the official showed him the cash. The inside of her entire outer jacket was quilted with cash. Astonishingly, 221 US one-hundred-dollar bills had been ingeniously stitched into her quilted jacket. The amount before Billy and the port official totaled $22,100. To the impoverished Korean descendants living in China, this was an enormous amount of money. In China, this gigantic amount equaled twenty years' wages.

Pastor Billy gladly received the money from the amazed official. When the time came closer to the promised date, back in China the church members could not sleep at night and eagerly waited in front of the radio, prayerfully listening. On the promised date and hour, the regular broadcast suddenly stopped. Billy's voice came flowing out from the radio.

"Dear fellow Christian brothers and sisters in China, we have received well the offering you all have sent to us." The moment they heard the broadcast, they exclaimed "Hallelujah!" as they hugged each other in tears. Five years later, those same Korean descendants in China sent another $8,000, along with a gold necklace and a gold ring, as an offering for the radio broadcast missionary work.

This is what one Korean descendant from one of those areas, from a congregation of the so-called FEBC Radio Church confessed: "It is not an offering that they give; it is the sacrifice of their lives that they give." Through this incident, Billy directly eyewitnessed churches that had been established wherever the FEBC broadcast was transmitted.

Miss Choi remained in Korea, and through the mediation of Pastor Billy Kim, married a deacon of the Suwon Central Baptist Church. After their marriage, her husband studied in a seminary and became a pastor. Currently, the couple works as missionaries living in China. Billy envisioned that someday, in North Korea, churches would be established through FEBC radio broadcasts.

LISTENERS IN NORTH KOREA

Pastors who had visited North Korea, like Pastor Sun Hee Kwak and Yong Jo Ha, relate that North Koreans have been secretly listening to the FEBC radio broadcasts. They take notes of sermons as well as hymns and share them with their brothers and sisters in Christ in their underground churches. Billy envisions family churches and underground churches being established wherever the FEBC broadcast is transmitted. Billy continues to hope and pray for this.

"God, who has raised the FEBC transmitting towers above the centers of materialism and atheism in Russia, please also raise a radio tower in Pyongyang, North Korea." Billy dreams of the establishment of FEBC-Pyongyang. He doesn't mind if it is established by someone else. If not Moses, Joshua is fine too.

"What is preached is the gospel of Christ, and even I am only a stepping-stone for such holy works. It is a blessing and honor," he confessed.

He marches forward, toward that distant grand dream.

MEET THE RIGHT PARTNERS

One day in 1964, Billy received a phone call from a physician. "Pastor, we need your help. I am having a difficult time opening a Christian hospital in Suwon."

"Christian hospital" along with the word "difficult" combined to challenge Billy's heart. There was nothing better than a Christian hospital for spreading the gospel. Establishing a medical missionary work was something Billy Kim had always wanted to do. Difficulties can always be overcome, he was convinced, when one seeks God's help and is diligent to do the work.

The physician explained his problem was finding the right partners. The physician had been considering the following doctors: a surgeon, obstetrician, ophthalmologist, an ear, nose, and throat doctor, etc.

"Are they all Christians?" Billy asked.

After a bit of hesitancy, he replied, "There are some who are not so deep in their faith, and there are those who have not yet started their walk of faith."

Having the right people was more important than establishing the work. Billy replied that he would help with establishing Suwon Christian Hospital, under the condition that all of the coworkers would first become faithful Christians.

Billy called all the doctors who were willing, asking them to attend a daily Bible study on the gospel of John. He wanted them not to be merely "coworkers" but "partners." He wanted them to be medical missionaries, able to take up the calling of an evangelist. The faith of the partners was most important.

SUWON CHRISTIAN HOSPITAL

As the Bible study continued, "Suwon Christian Hospital" hung its temporary sign on September 19. The hospital opened its doors, but the rooms did not have beds or even an ambulance. Everything was lacking. Billy went to Suwon and Osan Airports, and brought back any leftover beds. As for the ambulance, a fellow Bob Jones alumnus and missionary in Japan, Pastor Ron Blough, renovated his own vehicle and sent it. It was the first ambulance ever in Suwon.

In his following sabbatical year, Billy went to the United States to raise funds to build a new Suwon Christian Hospital. Many of the churches he visited were led by pastors with degrees from Bob Jones University who supported Billy, despite his censure by their alma mater. The schedule was strenuous, requiring Pastor Kim to travel across much of America. Nothing was impossible for God, who empowered him.

He overcame the difficulties in raising the funds by presenting a vision for the spread of the gospel to the patients. Whenever he became exhausted and tired, he set his mind on building the best medical facility in Korea, for people who did not have the money to receive treatment. God did not neglect Billy's prayers and efforts.

In 1965, on a lot size of .8 acre, a totally modernized medical facility, Suwon Christian Hospital, was built. The four-story structure provided 24,300 square feet for patient and lab services. People had told him that this would be impossible. During the dedication ceremony of the hospital, First Lady Young Soo Yoon, wife of President Jung Hee Park, personally attended and toured the large hospital.

Just as Billy vowed, the hospital provided free medical services to the destitute. In hopes that every patient would become blessed as a part of the family of faith, he gave Christians a 30 percent discount.

THE HOSPITAL CHAPLAIN

From the opening of the hospital, Billy did not interfere with hospital management but carried out his role as the hospital chaplain and immersed himself in spreading the good news of the gospel. Also he placed an assistant pastor, Moon Bu Oh, as permanent staff in the hospital, for counseling and comforting responsibilities. The *Christian News* reported on March 20 that year:

> In our review of the current work of evangelizing through the Suwon Christian Hospital, we have found that they have installed good-news handout racks, and keep them constantly replenished. The pharmaceutical [staff] pass out these good-news handouts as they distribute medications. They also distribute them directly to outpatients, and guide people who are interested to the consultation office. They provide faith counseling services and confirm many to the faith in Jesus Christ for their salvation. In addition, the hospital has begun playing hymn praises and Bible messages through its internal broadcast during break times. They visit any [patient] who needs comfort. Just last year, over 12,000 handouts were distributed to nearly 5,000 patients resulting in 314 new believers.

Billy had helped build a wonderful missions center called the Suwon Christian Hospital. As time passed, the hospital grew to become a complete facility, an equipped general hospital having physicians, surgeons, ophthalmologists, otolaryngologists, obstetricians, gynecologists, radiologists, laboratory pathologists, and physiotherapists. The hospital even included a blood-bank facility. At that time, there was no general hospital like Suwon Christian Hospital, and it soon became crowded with more than three hundred patients.

DIVERGING OPINIONS

However, its rapid growth and very size created several problems. Management could not agree on how to respond to the hospital's growing size, and many had strong, diverging opinions. They could not come to a consensus, and soon the managers went their separate ways. After just ten years of operation, Suwon Christian Hospital became a part of history.

On the day the hospital closed, Billy cried. He cried in pain, because a place for sharing the gospel had closed down. He cried because of losing the "partners."

In Billy's view, "A good partner is vital in gospel-centered management. A 'coworker' is someone who can leave anytime according to their interests. However, a 'partner' is someone who will remain forever for the gospel. Choose the right partners of faith."

CARING FOR THE ELDERLY

As Billy carried out the role of the vice-director on the board of directors of the Swanson Memorial Preservation Foundation, which had provided the FEBC-Korea base house, he also continually shared the gospel with the orphaned children. That was because it was the desire of the Korean orphans' "father," Pastor Swanson. However, in 1982, since the Swanson Memorial Preservation Building had become a private asset of Billy's, he faced concerns about what to do with it, since he was thinking of relocating the base house to Suwon.

Korea had already stepped up its economic performance, becoming the top-ranked nation among developing countries. Elder care was becoming a more critical social issue than orphan matters. On several occasions, Billy had received requests from the city of Suwon and its surrounding area for a much needed elder care home. Billy thought that building a home for the elderly instead of an orphanage was consistent with Pastor Swanson's vision.

Orphans and homeless elderly people were not much different from one another. They both desperately needed help. Both groups were isolated and often helpless. They both needed the joy of hearing the good news of the gospel, as well as comfort.

THE SUWON ELDER CARE HOME

Billy believed that the formality of the original Swanson Foundation Christian goals did not rule out helping the elderly. He was able to persuade the foundation representatives to construct an elder care home. In 1983, with $300,000, the home was built.

The partner in building this project, Pastor Yi Sun Baek, has remained the manager of that elder care home for more than thirty years. Pastor Baek first met Billy in November of 1967 when Billy had been the speaker at a "National Revival for Bible Teachers in Orphanages." Pastor Baek had been moved greatly during that event. Later he contributed to the establishment of the elder care home. He also married Billy's secretary, Miss Young Ja Choi. Pastor Baek recollects, "I cannot forget the day that I got engaged at Pastor Billy Kim's residence. Everything had been prepared by Pastor Kim and his wife, Trudy . . . everything, including food and clothing."

Billy visited the Suwon Elder Care Home whenever possible. He would hold residents' hands as he comforted each of the senior residents there. Over the years, Billy often gave his honorarium and lecture fees received from revivals and other events, without even opening the envelopes. Billy continually asked Pastor Baek for these three things: "Please serve them with good food. Please provide them with good clothing. Please take care of them so that they stay comfortable."

"I've always kept Pastor Billy Kim's three requests in mind, in taking care of the elderly folks," Pastor Baek once remarked. He noted Billy's example and heart: "Pastor Kim himself demonstrated [those three things] by his own actions. He wholeheartedly served all the elderly, as if they were truly his own parents."

A LARGER ELDER CARE HOME

Suwon Elder Care Home, the Swanson Memorial Preservation Foundation's social welfare organization, had grown into something worthy of close attention. As automaker BMW made plans to move into South Korea, leaders visited the site and surrounding land and realized it was a prime location for their headquarters. They offered $9 million for the land, and Kim and others agreed, seeing a great opportunity for God. They moved the elder care home to the countryside, where land was less expensive and the money would go further. In 2004, they completed construction of a larger, multilevel elder care facility, now called the Suwon Central Elder Care Home. With room for two hundred residents, today it includes an education center, rehabilitation and welfare center, resting place, and a place for spiritual growth.

The elder home had experienced steady growth, year after year, without any division among leadership over the previous twenty-eight years. Billy stated that "the growth of a small Suwon Elder Care Home into what it is today as the grand Suwon Central Elder Care Home was possible through the wonderful partnership with Pastor Yi Sun Baek, of the Swanson Memorial Preservation Foundation and American businessman Paul Johnson.[1] Being a partner means practicing without ceasing, to become one in the Spirit of the gospel."

CENTRAL CHRISTIAN ACADEMY

The remote location of the Kims' home had attracted many burglars. By the 1990s, however, the area had been developed and became the center of Suwon. For over thirty years, everyone had known the city as the place Pastor Billy Kim lived. Each pyeong (35.6 square feet) of the lot had been formerly valued at three cents, and now had become worth $3,000 per pyeong. Naturally, most people would want to keep it their own possession. However, Billy never once considered it as his own land and proved it by selling the land to help build the Central Christian Academy.

Located in Suwon, Central Christian Academy (CCA) was built on more than fifteen acres. The three floors and basement provided a massive 345,200 square feet. The lot alone cost $3 million, and the construction fee had been $7 million, for a total investment of $10 million dollars. To help with the purchase, a corporation paid for the lot, and Suwon Central

Baptist Church paid $3 million for the CCA's Christian Center, to use as an education center.

In addition, Billy took out his entire retirement pension of $100,000 in advance from FEBC-Korea. He also moved his father's burial site to another location and sold that lot for a profit of $200,000, which he contributed entirely to the construction costs.

The biggest partner in this endeavor was his wife. Trudy had started the Central Kindergarten in 1960, which would become the foundation for the Central Christian Academy. Central Kindergarten had grown to twelve separate classrooms and had become highly recognized throughout Suwon. Parents of graduating students kept asking for an elementary school to follow in the same traditions of this prestigious education.

Billy and Trudy, after having sold their house, had no place to live and moved into a ten pyeong (355 square feet) house that a janitor had resided in, next to the Christian Center. Trudy was delighted in doing so.

Billy's oldest son, Pastor Joseph Kim, was also a big partner. Joseph and his family moved into two small rooms on the second floor of the kindergarten teachers' dorm, for the next two and a half years. Joseph was the overseer at the construction site and was in the forefront of raising the necessary funds.

Central Christian Academy opened its doors in 1994. Today, CCA is praised for its large-scale construction. Its aesthetically sophisticated design suggests an art gallery or a museum. Billy, who had surrendered his entire life possessions for the construction of the academy, did not have any possession rights whatsoever. The academy was managed by eight corporate directors, and Joseph became the school's chaplain.

More recently, a middle school has been added to the elementary school. Just as Bob Jones has grades from kindergarten through graduate school, perhaps this will also occur at CCA. Perhaps one day a high school will be built, then a college, and then a graduate school.

Billy explained, "My wife is my best partner. My sons and my daughter, their spouses, along with all of my grandchildren, are my great partners. However, in this I confess, one must not have any selfish desires. There must not be any selfish motives. All that is required in a partner is to have the heart of our Lord God. It is God's heart, unsparingly giving love, while suffering on the cross. His heart was pierced, gushing out blood and water from extreme pain."

Part 3

THE ENERGIZER
SERVING IN HIS POWER

An energizing servant of God helps others to meet and serve a holy God. You and I can do this only with the power that comes from God's ultimate servant, Jesus Christ. Jesus served the physical and spiritual needs of all, but He would prepare Himself for ministry through time with His Father (see Matthew 14:14–23). So must we.

In part 3, we will learn the ways of energizing servants. They display a pure heart, a willingness to sacrifice, and grace to others (because of the grace shown them), and they have the message that is worth giving their energy to. And because they are close to me and have shown servant hearts through many years (passing the test of time), I will hold up two shining examples: my guardian, Carl L. Powers, and my closest friend (and wife), Trudy Stephens Kim.

12

SERVE WITH
A PURE HEART

Carl Powers, who had brought Billy to study in the United States during the Korean War, had a father who worked at the railroad doing manual work. His mother was a country farm housewife, who took care of a little land around her house and two cows. Carl's house was far away, deep in a rural area, quite distant from the village of Dante, Virginia. It was isolated from the rest of the world. He did not even have a well near his home.

During one summer vacation, Billy has memories of digging a water well and for the first time connecting a water faucet inside Carl's home. Even the bathroom had been outdoors. Billy, while still young, at times had taken care of his business in the middle of the night, through a small window in his room.

When Carl had decided to bring Billy to the States, Carl was only twenty-two years old. He was only six years older than Billy, like an older brother. Carl also needed to continue his studies at the university. His dream was to become a schoolteacher. He was having financially difficult times, barely managing to go to the university with an army scholarship. He certainly did not have the financial means to support a private high school's $750 annual tuition, for a student from Asia to whom he was not related in any way.

Carl even postponed getting married to support Billy. He tried hard to keep the promise he had made to Billy's mother that he would send Billy back home safely, after her son had finished his studies. However, he did not sacrifice for Billy only to keep his promise to Billy's mother. Carl considered Billy as his own brother, trusted Billy, and listened at times, following what Billy asked him to do.

CARL BECAME A CHRISTIAN

When Billy went back home to Carl during his first vacation, he told Carl, "I have accepted Christ." Immediately, Carl responded by saying, "I, too, will believe in Christ," promising that he would start going to a church. All this time, in spite of encouragements from everyone in his family to attend church, Carl had remained steadfast in not attending.

This is what Carl later wrote in a magazine: "All this time, I could not understand how I came to know a foreign boy and started supporting him. However, I know now that God wanted to give Billy a new 'word' through my help. God wanted the new 'words,' through Billy, to reach even the highest places under heaven, including the desolate, despairing people of Korea."

On Christmas Day 1978, while in the Holy Land, Billy baptized a man in the Jordan River. He was a bachelor and a teacher in a rural village in Virginia. Sergeant Carl Powers received baptism from his houseboy. Billy was moved beyond words as he baptized Carl, more than any others he had baptized previously.

In his memoir, *A Heart Speaks*, Carl Powers expressed his motivation in helping Billy in Korea and later Trudy and Billy in their ministry in Korea: "I shall always help you [Billy] and Trudy as much as I can materially, and I shall pray for you, [whether for] a minute, five minutes, or an hour—whenever my mind finds you."[1] Billy had always mentioned that for all Carl's assistance, there would be a crown in the heavenly kingdom waiting for him. As Carl wrote, "What I did for you was born and nourished by a sincere, abiding and activating love; love not of myself, but of God, which was in my heart moving me to act. . . . No thoughts of a heavenly crown colored my action. The least crown God had to offer is far too great for my unworthy head."[2]

Those words were truly like Carl. The first time Carl had met Billy, he was not yet a Christian. He had never expected anything from Billy or any religious rewards for his actions. He simply helped Billy. Carl served with a pure heart. One must serve with a pure heart.

SERVING EACH OTHER

Billy never forgot the serving by Carl's family. Carl's family consisted of his mother, father, and two brothers. Whenever Billy met with the family during his vacations, Carl's parents were delighted and considered him as their youngest son. They were really proud as they saw him adjust so well to American life.

Carl's parents did not repaint the basement wall or the stairway after Billy had returned to Korea, wanting to keep the fond memories of their youngest son. They kept all the letters from Billy, as well as the trophy he had won during his high school national speech contest. They even kept the actual live LP recording of the speech contest. They hung pictures of Billy and Trudy throughout their house.

Carl's brothers were musically talented, and when Billy made it to the university, they performed bluegrass on the street to collect money for Billy's tuition. Billy never forgot how much he was moved by it all. Their love for Billy was certainly that of true brothers. To return a little of their love, Billy, too, helped with any possible household chores, whenever he could.

Cutting the hay for the two cows was always Billy's chore. It was quite different from the ways back in Korea, so Billy had a hard time at the beginning. He went to the steep, mountain slopes and used a large sickle to reap the grass, dry it, roll it up after it dried, and then stack it neatly in the barn. It was only during his summer vacations, but still he helped with the laundry, washed the cars, and chopped the wood. Whatever he could do, even if it was only a small errand, he wanted to help. Billy was a part of Carl's family.

CARL'S LIFE OF SERVICE

Carl remained a bachelor in the rural area of Virginia for the rest of his life. He dated a woman for about four years. She had been introduced to Carl by Billy and Trudy, but because she did not want to live in such a rural village, they parted ways, and he remained single.

Carl was envious of Billy, thinking that if he had found a woman like Trudy, who was from an American middle-class family, and who married Billy knowing she would live in the impoverished land of Korea, he would gladly marry such a person too.

Yet there was a reason Carl chose not to leave his hometown and eventually gave up on marriage. His hometown village had a coal mine, and the impoverished children of that region must start working immediately after finishing middle school. As a teacher, Carl helped many of his students to complete high school—and he shared the gospel with them. He believed this was his lifetime calling. If there were students who wanted to continue their education in a university, he helped provide their tuition. He was truly a teacher who helped fulfill the dreams of many students and was like a father who took care of them until the end. Through Carl's sacrificial endeavors, many children from that village became wonderful, educated members of society.

After Carl accepted Christ as his Savior, his heart for service grew, and he sensed that Billy's love was born not primarily out of gratitude to his sponsor but a love for God. Carl now knew the divine source personally and in writing thanked the pastor for his godly influence: "As a friend tried and true you have exerted valuable and fruitful influence upon me. Your concern for even the little things in my life has touched me deeply and given me the feeling I am of some value yet. Indescribable is the joy I have experienced with you in drawing closer to Christ our Lord. . . . Thanks to your influence I am established more firmly in the Faith of our Fathers and in zeal to live for God."[3]

AN ACTIVE RETIREMENT

Carl officially retired in September of 1999. Nevertheless, he volunteered twice a week, serving at the Irvington Public School. He served reverently and humbly.

In June of 2000, fifty years after the Korean War began, the Korean station KBS2-TV aired a documentary called "Billy's Return to His Hometown." The producer, Eun Taek Lee, said, "Pastor Billy Kim called Mr. Carl Powers a saint, but when we went to the US to shoot on location, we were able to confirm that the town folks actually thought of him as a saint."

Sergeant Carl Powers went to be with the Lord on September 21, 2013. Billy recalls how he felt about Carl, the servant: "I have come to be where I am today through the help of others, my entire life. This is the reason why I want to live my life as a stepping-stone, for others to rise up. Carl wholeheartedly served his own houseboy. His dedication to serving has grown into the bigger serving of the nations. And at last, it bore the fruit of greatly serving the world. Herein lies the secret—a small service bears fruit in becoming a greater service. We should all continue to be servants until the day of our last breath."

Billy's servant heart was the result of Carl's heart of serving.

Billy Kim's lifelong friendship with Carl Powers influenced both men, from when Billy prepared for college (top left) to Carl's first return visit to Korea (top right) and beyond. Sergeant Carl took Billy's two sons on a boat ride during his first visit. Billy was moved beyond words when he baptized Carl and his own son John in the Jordan River.

The Kims welcome neighbors to their new home, and Trudy spends time with the deaconesses of their church. She becomes skilled at making kimchi, a Korean staple. She also serves with Billy at the Central Elder Care Home.

Trudy joins in the applause as Billy Kim is welcomed as the new president of the Baptist World Alliance on July 5, 2000.

Billy Kim continues to minister to the Korean and American military forces, beginning at home. He leads Korean soldiers in prayer services in a forest.

Dr. Kim preaches to the 2006 graduating class at the United States Air Force Academy. Earlier he prays privately with two cadets. Kim receives the Good Neighbor Award from the United States armed forces for his service to the military.

In Havana for his installation as president of the Baptist World Alliance, Dr. Kim meets with Cuban President Fidel Castro. The evangelist presents Castro a Spanish Bible, prompting Castro to say, "When I was young, my mother spent a lot of time reading the Bible to me."

In his prayers and through personal meetings, Dr. Kim supports leaders of many countries. He has met most former Korean presidents, including Myung Bak Lee, and former US Presidents Jimmy Carter, Bill Clinton, and George W. Bush.

One of Pastor Kim's joys has been preaching at united Easter services in his homeland, both in large arenas and outside stadiums. He continues to pray for unity in Korean churches and for a unified Korea—north and south—one day.

13

SERVING IS AN UNEXPLAINABLE SACRIFICE

Trudy's full name is Gertrude Stephens Kim, but everyone calls her Trudy. She was raised in a typical American middle-class family. Her father worked in an office, and her mother was a teacher. Her four siblings all graduated from Bob Jones University. Her oldest brother, Roland, was a surgeon and had worked as a missionary in Africa. Perhaps she dreamed of becoming a missionary to Africa ever since her school days because of this brother. If she had not been so open to missions, she probably would not have accepted a date with Billy.

Trudy was pretty, and not only was she popular among the boys, but she had dated the son of the school's president. But God had other plans for her, plans that would require an unexpected, even unexplainable, sacrifice.

It began with the letter by Billy and an assist by his English teacher (see p. 49). Two years later, with graduation from Bob Jones approaching, Billy would propose to Trudy during one date. "Trudy, I now must return to my homeland, and work for my impoverished fellow country-men. Would you go with me?"

Whether the answer was unexpected or unexplainable, Trudy answered without the slightest hesitancy, "Yes!" That one word was the biggest example of her "serving" heart she had shown to Billy to date. More would follow. Trudy would marry into a family of poverty in what was then a poor country. Those living in Korea then earned an average annual income of sixty-eight dollars.

AN EVANGELIST AND HOSTESS

Her first residence in Korea would be a household of fourteen family members, all living in a tiny three-bedroom, thatched-roofed house. Not only did she have to prepare food for up to fourteen people, but in addition, she had to boil feed for the cattle. Yet she devotedly cared for and served them, including her mother-in-law. She never complained.

During Trudy's six months living with Billy's oldest brother's family, her serving resulted in the wonderful fruit of evangelizing the entire family. There she also taught English conversation to college students during the two-month semester break. Trudy would sit on the warm floor of the living room with the students every afternoon for two or three hours. Some days she even made chocolate chip cookies for them. The home had no oven, but Trudy learned to bake a few cookies in a hot electric skillet with a lid over the small-sized cookies. Everyone who tried one of the cookies begged for more. Billy's seventy-five-year old mom was a great fan of these cookies.

Later, when they moved into their own house, she continued the free lessons in English and presented her Christian faith to those who asked. Some of her most impoverished college students lived with her at the house. Some students had been kicked out of their own homes for believing in Christ. Trudy took care of those students with a smile, as if they were her own children, and even supplied their personal necessities.

Pastor Daniel Lee, of Global Mission Church, was in awe of how Trudy could serve others so unselfishly. She had a reputation for making a truly "incomprehensible sacrifice."

In the last years of the 1960s, Trudy started the Central Kindergarten in Suwon. As enrollment and graduates increased year after year, the Central Kindergarten gained a reputation for its graduating students being more outstanding and creative. This became the foundational, motivating spirit behind Central Christian Academy.

Central Christian Academy had a swimming pool and many other sports, recreational facilities for the general public. Seeing an opportunity, Trudy opened a pie shop, called "Trudy's," where she baked fresh pies and cookies all day. A wonderful aroma lingered in and around the shop all day long! Trudy was known for her delicious, home-baked goodies, which former Korean presidents would recall from their occasional visits to the Ingyedong house.

However, baking cookies and pies at a pie shop for the public was quite different from baking fresh homemade goodies for a few. It was hard work, 365 days a year, struggling with flour and never having time to take off her apron. It required her to sweat for long hours in front of a hot oven. It mandated that she become a store clerk in addition to the hard work of having to produce goodies in response to the increasing demand.

Trudy voluntarily took on this additional difficult task, which would provide money for scholarships for the special handicapped children at the Central Christian Academy. At the same time, she needed to oversee her work as the superintendent of the Central Kindergarten. She was also the wife of a pastor of a nearly 15,000-member congregation, the Suwon Central Baptist Church.

Trudy also was the mother of three children, who at that time endured being teased for their racially mixed identity. Additionally, she had to attend various events as well as meet her husband's needs. Billy sometimes invited more than thirty guests to their home without giving prior notice. Not one of these roles seemed easy, but Trudy never complained.

ANOTHER NAME FOR SERVING IS LOVE

If she really wanted to provide scholarships for the tuition of the special needs children, she could have simply asked her husband for help, but she didn't. She baked with her own two hands to provide for those handicapped children. Trudy's, with its scents of warm cookies and pies, became a place to gather and have meaningful conversations.

Trudy delighted in her life of self-giving sacrifice. She delighted in serving with actions—not words. She wanted to go to the places in need and actually help, and not just talk about it. This was the biggest reason for Billy's admiration and respect for his wife.

And though she served her husband, whom she loved, ultimately she served Christ. Her motto has remained "for me to live is Christ"; her reminder "Christ lives in me" (Philippians 1:21; Galatians 2:20). Along the way, Trudy had become more Korean-like than her husband. She occasionally pointed out her husband's method of handling things by saying, "Billy, that is not the Korean way of doing things." Trudy truly loved the Korean people. She had become a Korean woman, who must have her daily kimchi, a tasty side dish made of cabbage, scallions, Korean radish, red pepper flakes, and various seasonings. She even loved the strong-smelling, fermented bean stews.

STOOPING TO PLUCK THE WEEDS

One boiling hot summer day, someone noticed Trudy stooping to pluck out weeds in the grass of the sports field. To protect herself from the sun, she had covered her head with a towel and was wearing typical Korean country style, ankle-cuffed, baggy pants. The person who saw her thought that Central Christian Academy was now hiring foreign laborers.

Billy's former secretary of FEBC-Korea, Ms. Shin Sook Kang, said of Trudy, "Once I went to the church bathroom, and was so shocked. Pastor Billy's wife, Trudy, was cleaning the bathroom by herself. Naturally, I felt reverent respect for her. It was not just on that one occasion, but I saw her cleaning the bathroom again—this time with her daughter-in-law. To lower one's self in humility can be easily said but is much harder to live it."

Trudy had always, in humility, served wholeheartedly through her actions. Her actions were those of serving Christ. One time Billy mentioned, "There have been times when people spoke ill of me, yet to this day, I have not heard anyone speak ill of my wife."

Jesus loved people. That is why He came to this world. To serve means to be with others, in their lowest places of life. It is to sincerely love and care for what others love to do.

It is to identify with others, with the same laughter or ways of speech. If asked to go five miles, it is to answer "Yes!" and willingly walk ten miles. Yes, to serve means to act in love. To serve is just another name for "love revealed in action." Trudy embraced the lifestyle of a servant in another land, and by her service would spread "the fragrance of the knowledge of [Christ] everywhere" (2 Corinthians 2:14).

14

SERVE WITH A GRACE-FILLED HEART

I n the middle of the Korean War, it was nearly impossible for an underage minor to enter the United States alone. Once Billy was ready to leave, his sponsor, Sergeant Carl Powers, was urgently called back to the most northern frontline unit before he could finish the necessary documentation for Billy's departure.

Left alone in the southern port of Pusan, his departure point for America, Billy had to try to process the complicated documentation on his own. Billy had gone to the US servicemen's help desk at the Pusan station, just as Carl had instructed him. However, no one had been willing to help the young boy, who was obviously not on any army duty. Further complicating things, no one dared to pay attention when he said, "I am here to process my papers to study abroad."

As Billy absentmindedly sat, like a worn-out sack of potatoes, a somewhat prankish looking soldier had said, "Hey kid, you have an older sis?" Billy remembered the picture he had in his bag of an older sisterlike person in Kyesung.

In a moment, he exhibited his wit. "Yup, do you wanna see my sis's picture?" She was actually the daughter of someone he knew, who used to work in the Kyungsan area as a laundry maid. She was pretty.

Suddenly, all the soldiers who had been negligent until that moment stood in line to help him with the documents. One of these soldiers was Bong Jik Han, a military police transport officer of the Military Transportation Command. He helped Billy with the papers, as they shared many stories together.

He treated Billy like his own brother and afterward arranged a train seat among the military police's designated seating for Billy's return to Suwon. The night before Billy's departure, they even had dinner together and watched a movie.

AN AFFINITY OF KINSHIP

Of course, Billy studied in the United States for the next eight years, while Bong Jik Han, after formally being discharged from his military duties, returned to his hometown in Gosung, Kangwondo, where he started a business selling dried fish products. Those products were sold in Suwon as well, and one day, several years later, Bong Jik Han's father planned to travel to Suwon and collect transaction payments.

When he learned his father would be in Suwon, Bong Jik asked his father to inquire about Billy there. It was 1962, and Billy had already become known in the Suwon region, so the father was able to quickly locate Pastor Billy. Hearing that his friend Bong Jik was looking for him, Billy immediately left for Gosung.

The two had not seen each other for ten years. Billy shared the good news of Christ Jesus. Bong Jik promised that he would attend a church nearby, with all of his family members. Afterward, whenever Han went to Seoul, he always visited Suwon on his way, and Billy, whenever he went to the Mt. Seorak area of Kangwondo, stopped by to visit in Gosung. Both built their bond of friendship far beyond their kinship in Christ.

REMEMBERING THE SMALLEST IN SERVING

One day, a call came from Gosung. It was Bong Jik Han's wife. "My husband has been called to God." Only age forty-eight, Bong Jik Han had died due to an accidental electrocution. Bong Jik's family was unprepared for funeral procedures after such a sudden death.

"Pastor, after we attended your mother's funeral, my husband wanted to be buried in your family's graveyard, if he was to die. Although this sounds quite out of the ordinary, I truly believe this is what he wanted." Billy was extremely busy with conference schedules, including the additional work of his church and the broadcasting work of FEBC-Korea. Still, he went straight to Gosung to facilitate the entire funeral process.

In addition, he asked his family's permission, and upon their approval, buried Bong Jik Han at his family's graveyard. Later, Billy helped Bong Jik Han's son to study abroad in the United States. The son graduated in the States and later became a pastor. True joy came as Bong Jik Han's son, Byeong Hyuk Han, worked with Billy, beginning in 1992, at the Suwon Central Baptist Church. Later, he became the head of FEBC-Ulsan and participated in the broadcast mission work.

Billy's acquaintance with Bon Jik Han during the Korean War was brief. Bong Jik Han's help during those Korean War days was precious, however, and Billy could not forget the transport officer's help.

A small favor done to Billy was for God's plan, and part of the return from such a small favor resulted in his burial in the same family graveyard, as if he had been part of Billy's family. It also resulted in Bon Jik's son working together with Billy as true partners in God. To serve is to be remembered. Billy knew his God does not forget even the smallest act of service. His followers are not to forego such acts of service. We are to serve with grace-filled hearts.

HOW TO RETURN A FAVOR

Billy never forgot the grace he received from God through Carl Powers. However, he felt he could not return the favor. Carl did not have plans to study overseas, nor did he want help with his living expenses. He didn't need anything, because he had no immediate family and had lived all his life as a bachelor. The only way Billy could return any favor was to do for others as Carl had done for him.

One person who had received help from Billy to study overseas in the United States had been Rev. John (Yong Pil) Song. After John graduated from high school, a former teacher introduced him to Billy. John would study at Hankuk University of Foreign Studies, majoring in English. His family had been so poor that he had worked as a shoeshine boy in his childhood. John had to leave college for the mandatory army duty in Korea, but when he returned to the university, he continued to have a hard time paying for his tuition.

John read an ad from the Osan Air Force labor recruitment department and then asked Billy to help him find a job. As usual, Billy had an extremely busy schedule but did not reject John's request. He went directly to Osan to speak to a major he knew well. The major introduced Billy to a deputy commander. Unfortunately, this did not result in employment for John.

Around six months later, John received a letter from a grandmother in the United States. Her name was Iric. After returning to his hometown in the States, the deputy commander, Colonel Barksdale, gave a testimony at her church. This was when she heard about Yong Pil's case—a student who desperately needed financial aid for further studies. She then decided to write to him. Through the help of this wonderful grandmother, Yong Pil was able to complete his studies at the university.

Unfortunately, the grandmother never got to see Yong Pil in person, because she was called to God. Later, whenever Billy went to the States, he took time to visit the son of "Grandma Iric" in Florida, and this continuing relationship had made it possible for Yong Pil to continue his studies at Bob Jones University School of Business, with the continued support from the family.

During his years at Bob Jones, Yong Pil married a Korean girl named Kye Shim Park, who had been studying education there. Her father, Tae Hyun Park, was the renowned composer of "Samiljeol" (March 1st Independence Movement Day), "Hangul Day" (Korean Alphabet Day), "Wind Blowing on the Mountain Top" (Korean Lied), and "Taegeukgi" (the national flag of Korea). Yong Pil had his own success as a certified public accountant (CPA), and Kye Shim and he were living a comfortable life with a relatively high annual income.

One day, Yong Pil and his wife simultaneously realized during their prayer time, "We did not come to the United States to earn money but for the sake of the gospel. What we are doing now seems unpleasing to God. Let's return to Korea and live our lives for the sake of the good news."

Yong Pil entered a seminary and later graduated as a pastor. He briefly ministered in the States and then returned to Korea to serve alongside Billy, who had made this all possible. He wanted to return the favor from Billy, if even in a small way. Pastor Yong Pil (John) Song served as the vice president of FEBC-Korea and later worked as the head of the FEBC-Los Angeles branch office. Later, he became the vice president of Torch Trinity University Graduate School of Theology. He was always ready to serve Billy, whenever there was a need. He is truly someone who repays even the smallest kindness, without forgetting to be deeply thankful.

SHOWING A GRACE-FILLED HEART

A grace-filled heart prompted Billy to help a woman learn English and study abroad, and a man take the stage and earn an education. Youngae Kim, a Korean living in China, was greatly moved while listening to the FEBC program and wanted to live a life of faith in Korea. She decided to come to Korea with her daughter, Hwa Kyung Lim. After arriving, she sought out Pastor Billy Kim. Billy helped the daughter to work in the FEBC-Korea Chinese language part of the broadcast. He later helped Hwa Kyung to acquire the English language. With support from Billy and President Bowman of FEBC International, Hwa Kyung Lim was later able to study abroad in the United States, where she received a doctorate degree.

A famous Korean pop singer, Young Nam Cho, became acquainted with Billy when he visited the Suwon Central Baptist Church during his army-duty break times. Whenever possible, he would sing a special praise song at the church. During the 1973 Billy Graham Crusade in Seoul, Saturday night had been dedicated to the army soldiers, and Young Nam

Cho sang a solo. Young Nam Cho, after completing his army duty, was able to go to Trinity Seminary in the United States, with help from Billy and Baptist pastor Rev. Kenneth Moon.

Young Nam Cho wrote in his collection of essays called "Nolmen, Nolmen,"

> When I look back, I'm not sure why I was so fortunate to receive so much attention from Pastor Billy. What I am sure of, is that Pastor Billy has done his utmost for me. Pastor Billy was just that type of person. Perhaps because he received help from so many others, he is so considerate of others as well. As I traveled in the United States, to places like New York, Chicago, Philadelphia, Washington, D.C., and Los Angeles, I met many students who indicated that they were able to study abroad because of an arrangement made by Pastor Billy Kim.

The only way Billy could repay Carl for all the grace he received was to facilitate the dreams of other indigent young people by sponsoring a gift to study abroad in the United States. The grateful pastor-evangelist did it often.

15

SERVE AS A
STEPPING-STONE

From the beginning of his return to Korea, Billy Kim had focused on evangelizing young people and then helping them to become faithful Christians. In December 1960, one year after returning to his homeland, he established Youth for Christ (YFC) ministry in Suwon. It became the forerunner of YFC-Korea.

YFC had been started in 1946 by Pastor Torrey Johnson of Chicago to reach wandering youths after World War II through weekly Saturday evangelistic youth rallies. These rallies were held throughout the United States, and YFC later became a world youth missions organization. Billy Graham, as a student, had attended these YFC rallies, and Billy Kim had also attended during his Bob Jones Academy years.

In Korea, missionary Chi Su Kil of TEAM had already begun working toward establishing a YFC-Seoul chapter in 1959. In 1966, with Chi Su Kil and Billy playing the key roles, YFC-Korea would begin, with Billy as the first president.

YFC-Suwon held many evangelistic rallies on Saturday nights, renting high school multipurpose halls. During these rallies, many US YFC praise teams, like "Teen Team," visited, opening the doors for Korean young people to experience world praise music, as well as providing an opportunity to hear prominent guest speakers. They also hosted various other programs such as quizzes, plays, seminars, and sports activities.

In the then-rural city of Suwon, junior and high school young people did not have any cultural opportunities. The YFC program gave these students a refreshing stimulus, and at times the rallies exceeded one thousand students. The Holy Spirit moved like fresh dew upon these young people, causing many to come to Christ in total surrender, with hands raised high.

RETURNING TO AMERICA FOR THE SUWON YFC

Billy, awed at this beautiful sight, prayed to God, "Lord, what can I do for these young people?" In the middle of his prayer, the Holy Spirit moved upon his heart. He had an order from above to provide a facility where these youths could openly and freely praise and worship God.

Toward the end of 1965, Billy returned to the United States at the beginning of his sabbatical year to raise funds for a Christian center in Suwon to help Youth for Christ reach out to area youth. With him were his wife, Trudy, and their five-year-old son, Joseph, and newly born daughter, Mary Kay. (Their younger son, John, was not yet born.) As they traveled to one place that "might" help, if some other place called for him to come right away, Billy turned the car around, and no matter how far, drove straight there.

He borrowed a Volkswagen Beetle from Trudy's brother Herb, which he knew to use the least gas. On this fundraising campaign, not every church would approve an invitation. In the process of searching for places that he thought might help, he might drive halfway and then receive a call to learn "no visit is permitted"; sometimes he had to reverse direction. In the process, the family traveled across the entire United States three times.

It had been a huge trip, taking a total of eight months. At times, they drove sixteen hours straight in order to save the $20 motel expense. The family's home became the car, where they slept, ate, drank, and rested.

God gave him an amazing dream each time he was exhausted and worn out. Sometimes he had visions of wandering youths coming forward as they lifted their hands high, shedding tears of repentance. At other times he saw visions of young people dedicated to the Lord and passionately praising Him in the newly built facility. He was able to visualize enormous numbers of the next generation of heavenly warriors being educated and trained to become the army of Christ, marching into the world. As a result of this trip in the United States, he was able to raise $200,000, a huge sum in a huge trip to fulfill a huge dream.

SUWON'S CHRISTIAN CENTER

The following year, as soon as he had returned to Korea, he purchased a 1,000 pyeong (.8 acre) lot and began construction of the Christian Center. However, the funds raised in the US still were not nearly sufficient. During the construction he raised additional funds. Suwon Central Baptist Church, along with Waldo Yeager of Christian Service and many fellow believers, both in and out of the country, contributed to this project. He even asked the YFC students to participate in the fundraising.

Billy always thought it to be a great virtue to be "debt free," so he wanted to build the Christian Center without debt. The students caught the vision. They sold newspapers, baked and sold sweet potatoes and peanuts on the streets, and gave the profits as an offering. Whenever possible, students came to help at the construction site to pass bricks, etc. With great effort from everyone involved, the Christian Center was completely built within a year.

The Christian Center was two stories, with 14,200 square feet for the teens; the ground floor featured an indoor gymnasium. The center became a landmark of community pride, not only to the Christian community but to the greater Suwon area, and its construction received great attention from the Gyeonggido province. The following report appeared in the *Gyeonggi Commerce and Industry* newspaper:

> Even though the city of Suwon belongs to the Provincial Government, it did not have an indoor gym facility, which inhibited the development of sports in Suwon. Through the Christian Service Committee's Korean representative, Rev. Jang Hwan Kim's efforts, along with

the erection of the Christian Center, an indoor gymnasium has now become available. This will significantly contribute to the development of sports in the city of Suwon. The gymnasium seats two thousand spectators. The center is also equipped with modern facilities including offices, a library, an auditorium, a restaurant, and a lounge area. The grand structure will not only contribute to the development of sports in Suwon but will also serve as a missions center, to spread truth and peace, as well as love and service. It will be instrumental in bringing the gospel to young souls and provide a place where valuable fellowship and other social services will occur.

ALWAYS DELIGHTED AT THE SEEING

With the completion of the Christian Center, the YFC rallies flourished. Numerous young people visited the center. Over two hundred of those YFC-Suwon teenagers would become pastors. One of those is Pastor Daniel Lee of the Global Mission Church.

Daniel Lee had initially visited a YFC rally purely out of curiosity about Pastor Billy Kim. He had a lot of interest in philosophy. Daniel saw this man who spoke English well, drove an American car, and had an American wife, and he wanted to learn English from this successful person, "Jang Hwan Kim." At that time, Billy was teaching English and Bible to the YFC students.

In the beginning, Daniel studied English and was only a spectator, snooping around the Bible study classrooms. Two Korean proverbs describe what happened: "You get soaked under a drizzle" and "Many drops make a flood." It took Daniel two years. He would ask difficult questions during the Bible study and roam around the outer surface of the truth of the gospel. However, as he started to read the Christian books given to him by Billy, he began to show interest in the person of Jesus Christ.

Just prior to enlisting in mandatory army duty in Korea, Daniel came to accept Christ into his life, while reading a verse from the Bible. "I do not set aside the grace of God, for if righteousness could be gained through the law, Christ died for nothing!" (Galatians 2:21 NIV).

He lived the life of a faithful believer during his time in the army, and after completing his army duty, he decided to work as a servant of God. He started as assistant administrator of YFC. Dr. Tae Kook Kang, who had graduated from Bob Jones, recommended that he study at the Korean Bible University. Daniel studied while still working. Later, he married Pastor Billy Kim's secretary, Myeong Ja Woo, who was also one of the YFC assistant administrators.

However, Daniel still found it hard to accept the biblical, theological principles, and this caused Billy's heart great sadness, as he watched him wander. Billy suggested that Daniel go overseas to the United States, to study theology. Once again, Billy decided to ask his adoptive father, Elder Waldo Yeager, for help. Even before Daniel, many other YFC students had been sent to him.

Daniel lived at Elder Yeager's residence while attending Detroit Bible College (now William Tyndale College). He adjusted well to studying and living abroad, and there he saw the true God. During the graduation ceremony he received the highest award as a preacher. He was ordained as a pastor in the United States, and after he returned to Korea in 1975, he worked as an assistant pastor at Suwon Central Baptist Church and also served as the general manager of YFC for two years.

After that, he became the pastor for the Church on the Hill in Seoul and then served the Seoul Baptist Church for four years, before returning to the United States to study for a doctorate degree. As he studied in the States, he established an organization called "Korean Students All Nations" (KOSTA), which now exists all over the world, doing great works of God internationally. Later he became the main pastor of Global Mission Church in Seoul.

HELPING FUTURE EVANGELISTS, PASTORS, AND SINGERS

Another pupil of Billy's early ministry was Jin Su Hwang, who had participated in the April 19, 1960, student protest against the dictatorial government. As a result, he was jailed. Billy visited the jail as part of his evangelistic outreach, and there he met Jin Su. The young protester had been the president of the Samil High School student body, as well as the head of the Suwon High School Alliance.

Jin Su was released after a week without being indicted. However, he had voluntarily dropped out of school and had nowhere to go. Billy brought Jin Su to his home, and he lived at the house until he graduated from high school—and remained with the Kims until he had graduated from the Korean Bible University.

Jin Su helped Billy at the church and also with evangelistic work at the hospital, at farming and fishing villages, at YFC, and at various other places. He later became a Presbyterian pastor and he is now serving as the main pastor of Jaeil Sungdo Church in Seoul.

One student of the early Bible classes held at the house, Young Kyun Ahn, accepted Christ while in the ninth grade, having heard the gospel from Billy. He was baptized one year later and vowed to become a pastor "like Pastor Billy." He often confessed, "Pastor Billy has completely changed my life." He became pastor of the Philadelphia Korean Baptist Church and noted the example of Mrs. Kim as well: "I've learned a lot from watching Mrs. Trudy, making gruel of beans and straw for cattle, while piggybacking her baby." He tried to follow her ways.

Professor Sul Ja Hong of the Korean Bible University was also a pupil from Billy's early Bible study group. During her Suwon Girls High School years, she was popular among the students because she was known to sing well and to act in various plays. She wanted to major in voice after she graduated from high school, but faced with her family's opposition, she gave up her dream. Billy hired her as his secretary and helped her enter the Korean Bible University. When her family found out about her entrance to a seminary, they kicked her out of the house. She then started living in the mission office and eventually with the Kims. Billy arranged a scholarship through a Mr. Larson in the United States, so that Sul Ja could continue her studies.

She would study during the weekdays at the seminary in Seoul and then would return to Suwon on weekends, to teach Korean to Trudy and to help at YFC by translating English praise songs into Korean. She earnestly tried to assist Billy and Trudy in any way in their ministries.

Praise songs translated by Sul Ja during those days include "I've Got Peace Like a River," and "I've Got Joy Down in My Heart." These songs were nationally aired on FEBC-Korea's program called "Youth Time," which had been produced and run by Billy, resulting in those praise songs becoming well known. Gospel praise songs were first introduced to Korea in this way.

Not long after Sul Ja graduated from the Korean Bible University, Trudy gave her the initial tuition money and the admissions papers to Stone College in Michigan. Billy further helped her to receive aid, not only for her tuition but for allowances as well, through Mr. Roy Castle in the States, enabling her to study music missiology. Sul Ja Hong launched three CDs while studying abroad in America, held several concert tours, and participated in conferences with Billy, giving her testimony and singing.

Many other people, in addition to those mentioned, have reaped the fruit of Billy's early ministry. Renowned pop singer Young Nam Cho has said, "It's impossible to list all those who have been helped by Billy to study abroad in the United States."

If Billy could do any small thing, he would gladly help, in any way possible, to become a stepping-stone for others. Billy once said, "I don't know why I loved them so much. I myself am at a loss for words as to why I was so sacrificial toward them. All I know is that I also received love and service from others, without any apparent reason whatsoever. Then he added, " I am so happy whenever I see my former students. Just as I was to them, I see that they too are striving hard to become stepping-stones for others."

Pastor Kim says giving birth to another server means going through "labor pains." But the result of serving another is to birth another server. And that is his goal. "I continue to want to be a stepping-stone for others. I want to be a stepping-stone for others to reach their dreams," he says, and to be effective servants in God's kingdom.

16

SERVE FOR
THE GOSPEL

Why do you meet and serve people from the highest stature to the lowest of positions?"

Billy answers unfalteringly, "To share the gospel."

Every year on Thanksgiving Day, at the Suwon Public Stadium, Billy hosts a big feast to serve elderly folks living in senior homes, street cleaners, soldiers, riot police, etc. Each year, many have been moved by this never-changing, wholehearted service. Among them, there are those who have accepted Christ. This is only one example of how Billy has always been fair and unbiased in serving people, whatever their social or financial status.

Not much is said about Billy serving in isolated places, or his service to people in lower social and economic conditions, but there is a lot said about him serving people of higher social status. Billy has kept exceptionally close ties with successive presidents of Korea: Chung Hee Park, Doo Hwan Chun, Tae Woo Roh, Young Sam Kim, Dae Jung Kim, and Moo Hyun Roh. Through the July 2009 edition of *Shindongah* monthly magazine (the oldest Korean current events magazine, in print since 1931),

Billy was once again known to the public as "President Myung Bak Lee's mentor—Pastor Billy Jang Hwan Kim." Billy became known as a political pastor.

POLITICAL PASTOR

Jesus Himself was labeled a "tax-collector's friend," because Jesus befriended the tax collectors who were disliked for extorting their own people and gaining wealth and power from them. Similarly, Billy Kim encountered politicians and presidents, and he saw their pain as he met them. He realized their anguish and afflictions. He empathized with their turmoil and aloneness in decision making. Billy felt their need for encouragement and comfort.

If every Korean pastor avoided befriending government leaders and was afraid of being labeled as a political pastor, then who could share the gospel with them? Whether currently or previously in power, he knew they were no greater than common men and women and had the same needs.

There is no one so poor as to not require love. Likewise, there is no one so rich as to not require love. They all desperately need God's love as much as anyone, reasons Billy. They, too, desperately need the salvation of the cross and the forgiveness of sins.

Billy has had his own principle for evangelizing politicians and corporate CEOs, and it is God-centered, not self-centered. Consider its effectiveness in spreading the gospel. *If you evangelize the president, then, perhaps it is easier to evangelize the state cabinet members. If you evangelize the parent,* he reasons, *it is easier to evangelize their children. If you evangelize the heads of large corporations, then, perhaps it is easier to evangelize the entire staff.*

It is a simple principle. The gospel should be shared with everyone. It is a big mistake to think that the good news should be shared only with the poor. Christ's love should be shared not only with the shepherds but also with the king. An evangelist is called to preach the gospel to everyone, because Christ came to save everyone.

Billy was certainly not a pastor with a political agenda. If he had been, he would have accepted the nomination from numerous former Korean presidents to run as a congressman. Instead, he once said with a smile, "A pastor has greater power than any the world has to offer."

Billy frequently met with politicians who had already left office. Some of them had been imprisoned for various reasons. A few of them were very much disliked and disapproved of by the public. Billy understood that meeting with such former politicians could put him in a negative light as well. However, to Billy, the important fact was not how one is viewed by the public. Rather, it is that one gives to the fallen, the isolated, and the neglected the good news of the gospel they so desperately need.

Billy would continuously meet politicians or CEOs without being selective in any way in order to share the gospel and to offer prayers and words of comfort. His heart was always ready to obey the command to share the gospel.

PRESIDENT CHUNG HEE PARK
AND RELIGIOUS FREEDOM

President Chung Hee Park's beliefs were close to Buddhism, and he had a strong inclination toward Confucianism, traditionally serving the family ancestry.

In the mid-1970s, the issue of having the US Army troops remain stationed in the Republic of Korea was stirring up controversy within America. During those times, Billy, together with the chairman of Byucksan Co., In Deuk Kim, tried hard to calm the rising US public opinion against South Korea, and fought since 1974 the withdrawal of US troops stationed. Several congressmen were publicly discussing issues of pulling out the US soldiers from Korea, because of Korea's humanitarian problems and prevalent religious oppression.

The situation intensified when Pastor George E. Ogle, who had spent ten years as a missionary with Urban-Industrial Mission (UIM), said to the American press, "Korea does not have religious freedom." He had been deported from Korea without further visa extension, for causing labor movements inside corporations.

John Chancellor, the anchor of *NBC Nightly News*, requested Pastor Billy Kim to appear on his show for an open, though abbreviated, discussion about these issues with Pastor Ogle. Pastor Kim had become known to the American public through the Billy Graham Crusade in Seoul, which had aired throughout America a few months earlier. However, NBC planned to have Pastor Ogle appear together with another Korean, who was in line with his opinion, whereas, Billy was to appear alone. Billy requested to have another person appear with him as well, in the interest of fairness, which the broadcast approved. Coincidentally, there was a missionary to Korea from the Holiness Church denomination who had just returned to the States for her sabbatical year of rest. Billy asked this missionary, Elma Kilborn, to appear with him. This was Billy's assertion,

> I have recently interpreted for the Billy Graham Crusade in Seoul, where over one million people gathered openly. This would be utterly impossible in a nation that does not have religious freedom. I also personally run the Christian radio broadcast called the Asia Radio Broadcast, which airs on 250 KW radio. We transmit Christian programs throughout the Korean nation daily. We also reach China, North Korea, Russia, Mongolia, and Japan with the gospel. Considering that the major radio broadcast stations in the United States have an average radio frequency of 100 KW, our Christian broadcast power is 2.5 times greater in Korea. How would such a powerful radio frequency be allowed in a country that has no religious freedom? I would like to make one point clear—there is no religious oppression in Korea. That does not mean that President Chung Hee Park is 100 percent great on every issue. All I ask is that people view Korea in the light of Korea's current economic reality, when considering religious freedom. I am asking, please do not view Korea from the same standpoint of the socially, economically, and politically stable United States. I am asking people to please view Korea from the perspective of an impoverished nation's president, who is trying hard to make a difference in the lives of its people, who are suffering from starvation. He wants to just provide the basic guarantee of their very lives.[1]

He emphasized that Korea was, by no means, a less developed nation. In addition, the Holiness Church missionary, Elma Kilborn, who appeared with Billy on that TV show, clearly pointed out the misjudgment of Pastor Ogle by saying, "I have lived as a missionary for the past forty years in Korea, and have never once experienced any oppression or restrictions, based on religion."

Through that TV show, many Americans came to understand that Pastor Ogle did not suffer from religious oppression but was being restricted from Korea for socially stirring up labor disputes through the Urban-Industrial Mission. After this incident, Billy toured the States, publicly campaigning for Korea. He did this voluntarily, spending his personal money, flying around America without being asked by the Korean government, and becoming a spokesperson for Korea.

BILLY KIM AND THE PRESIDENTS

Billy Kim never desired to be political, but like his American counterpart, Billy Graham, he sought to influence presidents to know Christ and have wisdom that would lead them to make right decisions for their country. Kim became close to President Chung Hee Park when President Jimmy Carter scheduled a visit to Korea in 1979. At that time, there was no one in the Korean government who had any relationship with the US president. However, Billy had personally met Jimmy Carter while he was the governor of Georgia through a revival conference, and they had remained friends. Because of this relationship, Billy had prayed a lot for Governor Carter when he ran for the presidency. Unfortunately, after Jimmy had become the president, the ties between the United States and Korea had weakened.

President Carter did not want to provide any diplomatic aid to Korea, even as an allied nation, because President Park was running a severe, dictatorial government. For various reasons, the relationship between the United States and Korea remained frozen. Now, as the 1979 presidential visit approached, President Carter was planning to use the threat of the removal of US Army troops as a means to resolve human rights issues under the military dictatorial government.

The relations between the two leaders got off to an icy start. President Carter refused the offer from the Korean president to stay at the Korean government's guesthouse, the Blue House; instead he lodged with the US soldiers at the army base. In response, President Park expressed his strong disapproval of the interference in domestic human rights issues by a foreign nation. The initial summit meeting between the two heads of state was moving toward certain disaster.

Recognizing the tension, President Carter asked, through then Korean Ministry of Foreign Affairs, to meet with the religious leaders of the nation. All religious leaders were invited to the Blue House Reception Hall, including Billy and his wife. When Trudy entered the Blue House, all the security guards gave her a friendly greeting. This was because Trudy had been teaching English to the Blue House special security guards twice a week.

Then the two presidents entered the reception hall, and President Park fixed his attention on Trudy as he entered. When asked later, the president replied that he had heard that Billy had married a foreign lady and was curious to see her.

A moment later, the attention turned to Billy, because President Carter's wife, Rosalynn, had given Billy a hug as soon as she saw him. All who attended watched, curious to find out who this person was that the US president's wife was eager to hug.

The following morning, President Carter invited ten religious leaders to the American embassy in Korea for a time of conversation. The first words from the president were, "I would like my friend to speak first." He was indicating Billy. It might have seemed impolite to the others, but because it was the request of the US president, Billy spoke first. Following in order were Pastor Kyung Chik Han of the Youngnak Presbyterian Church, and then Cardinal Stephen Sou Hwan Kim.

Cardinal Kim asked, "Are you aware, sir, that because of your visit to Korea, Young Sam Kim and Dae Jung Kim are under house arrest?"

President Carter replied, "I am sorry."

SPIRITUAL COUNSEL TO THE PRESIDENT

After the meeting, President Carter asked Billy to accompany him to the Yoido Baptist Church. Without any precedent for protocol, Billy went with Jimmy and his wife, along with their daughter, to the worship service. Billy mentioned in the car, "I am trying to evangelize President Park. Please help me. President Park is not an ill-willed person. He is a great patriot. I've kept President Park in my prayers, especially to share the gospel. I believe it would be better for you, President Carter, to evangelize him, than myself."

During the worship service, an urgent call came from President Park's chief bodyguard, Ji Chul Cha. He was asking Billy Kim to come immediately to the Blue House, after he was finished with President Jimmy Carter. It was Sunday, and a second summit meeting was scheduled to be held at 4 p.m. Prior to the meeting, President Park wanted to know what conversation took place in the car, between President Carter and Billy. The worship service had ended twenty minutes earlier, and Billy and President Carter sat on small stools in the church kindergarten, sharing personal updates over tea.

Jimmy Carter left for the National Assembly building, and now Billy went straight to the Blue House. Billy shared with President Park exactly what had been discussed in the car, and advised, "Please respond favorably, when President Carter shares the gospel with you. Then, I believe, you will have a good result from the summit meeting." The second round of the summit meeting ended successfully. As if to prove that things had indeed gone well, President Park and President Carter sat side by side in the car, on the way to the airport.

In 2001, former president Carter returned once again to Korea, to an area called Onyang. The purpose was to build a house of love through the Habitat for Humanity project.

The governor of Gyeonggi province, Mr. Chang Ryol Lim, contacted Billy, saying that Jimmy Carter wanted to meet with him. Billy went straight down to the province to meet him, and they ate an assortment of kimchi and rice together. Jimmy asked Billy, "Do you suppose, twenty years ago, when I shared the gospel with President Park in the car, as you asked, that he actually believed in Christ and is now in heaven?"

Billy told the president he could not be absolutely positive that President Park fully understood what it meant to trust in Christ as Savior and Lord. But Park did listen intently, Pastor Kim reminded the president.

It was admirable that former president Jimmy Carter did not forget, all this time, about a soul he had evangelized and might have led to trust in Jesus Christ. Whether President Park is in heaven, no one knows. If President Park had accepted Christ as his Savior through the witness of President Carter, he would surely have been saved.

All that one can do is to scatter the seeds of the gospel. The only one who can bear fruit, or reap from it, is God.

THE EVANGELIST AT A BUDDHIST TEMPLE

For Billy, meetings with presidents were never for comfort or recognition. Nowhere is this more obvious than with his rendezvous with former president Doo Hwan Chun in December 1988. Billy drove toward Baekdamsa, a Buddhist temple, leaving his home at 4:30 a.m. Deep winter fog blocked his view as he entered the east province of Kwangwondo. As he arrived at the grounds of the temple around eight o'clock, an armed security guard ran toward him from the guard post.

"Hello, I am Pastor Billy Kim." The guard had a confused look on his face at seeing a pastor at a Buddhist temple. Billy spoke with a sterner voice than usual. "I am here to pray for him." Faced with such an authoritative tone of voice, the guard went back to the post and made several calls to find out what was going on. Finally Billy got out of the car.

The fresh, cold air of Mt. Seorak awakened his tired body. As he entered the area of the shrine, he was flooded with camera flashes.

"What brings you here?" asked the reporters who monitored the former president's daily moves. Chun had been out of the presidency since February and had retreated to the monastery. Kim did not answer the question and walked straight forward. He could sense what the reporters were saying behind his back. "Political pastor." Then they added, "Pastor, you are the first non-Buddhist visitor, ever."

Again, Billy did not respond. Soon President Doo Hwan Chun and his wife gave him a friendly greeting. The room had a basin of water, warming over the heated ondol floor, which had been stained charcoal black from the heat. A wooden plank placed over a stack of bricks was being used as a dresser. Without being aware of it, Billy observed with interest every corner of the room.

"I used to live like this during my military cadet years."

The former president handed a floor cushion to him and looked over to the door flap. "A freezing draft penetrates through the gap. We've managed to cover it with a plastic sheet, which has made it noticeably better."

"You both look at ease." He couldn't think of any other words to comfort them.

"It's because I am being loved," First Lady Soon Ja Lee spoke with a soft smile. "When I have to go to the bathroom outside, in the middle of the night, my husband follows me with a flashlight. It's not often you receive guard protection directly from the president himself."

President Chun changed the subject, seemingly embarrassed. "On our way to Baekdamsa temple, we drove around in Suwon to avoid reporters. We remembered visiting your house for dinner with our son, Jae Kook, in the 1980s and thought, 'Pastor Kim's house is somewhere near here.'"

Billy's heart was moved. He talked for a long while with the former president and his wife. As the conversation seemed to be drawing to a close, he opened the pages of his Bible.

"For God so loved the world that he gave his one and only Son, that whoever believes in him shall not perish but have eternal life. For God did not send his Son into the world to condemn the world, but to save the world through him" (John 3:16–17 NIV).

Billy knelt and wholeheartedly prayed for the couple's salvation, as well as their comfort. In consideration that it was a Buddhist temple, he did not sing any hymns. The clock had turned to twelve noon. "I should be on my way."

President Chun grabbed Billy's hands as he was about to get up. "Pastor, please, you must have lunch with us in the temple." It seemed coldhearted to refuse their offer, and so he ate with them, the food prepared by the Buddhist monks. He left Baekdamsa, promising them that he would visit them again, with his wife, Trudy.

A few days later, as promised, Billy revisited Baekdamsa with Trudy and brought some homemade food. "People I have appointed as state ministers, and some with star ranks, try hard to avoid me, but you, Pastor

Kim, someone who doesn't owe me anything, write encouraging letters and send rice and other food. It seems like I am beginning my life all over again, after coming to Baekdamsa."

Billy was not a foolish person. As a pastor and CEO of a large broadcasting company, he knew well how the world works. He understood what was profitable and what was not. He knew that broadcast and press reporters, from both in and out of Korea, were surrounding the Baekdamsa area just to get a glimpse of former president Chun's life. When Billy told people that he would be visiting Baekdamsa for various reasons, they all tried to dissuade him.

Still, he went to Baekdamsa. His reason was simple. There was a soul there who needed to hear God's gospel.

Even if he must be permanently labeled as a political pastor, even if he had to endure some type of hardship in his broadcasting company as a result, and even if he was to take reproach from the majority of Korean people who disliked President Chun and his wife—he must go. In order to share the gospel, he would go anywhere.

THE BUDDHIST AT A BAPTIST CHURCH

Eleven years had passed since Billy had visited Baekdamsa.

Then, on December 25, 1999, former president Chun came to attend the Christmas worship service at the Suwon Central Baptist Church. Billy would never forget how moved he was that day. It didn't mean that the former president became a Christian. Pastor Kim simply understood it as a small reward, from long years of zealous effort, for the calling of a gospel evangelist. He was so delighted to see the former president, always responding with an "Amen" after each prayer and occasionally during Scripture reading.

After this, Billy noticed that the former president would occasionally come to participate in the worship. Billy continued to pray that the former president and his wife would become Christians.

Those visits happened during the FEBC-Yeongdong tower relocation from Mt. Obong to Mt. Kwebang, in May 2001, with which the former president assisted. To transmit a clear radio frequency of the gospel to the

North Korean lands far and near, the location of Mt. Kwebang was absolutely essential. The relocation site of Mt. Kwebang had been previously used for a Buddhist temple, and therefore was land reserved by Buddhist leaders. To obtain legal rights to use the land, Billy had met with the chief Buddhist monk, who represented ownership of the lot, but had been unsuccessful. It was understandable for the Buddhist monks not to allow the land to be used for spreading the gospel of Christianity. Many offers had been made by other radio broadcasting companies for this prime location but all had been flatly denied. Would it be any different for FEBC?

At this point former president Chun came to Billy's aid. The former president had a friendly relationship with the chief Buddhist monk throughout his everyday life, and with the former president's intercession, the temple lot was given up, for use as the FEBC-Yeongdong tower site. Billy's service to others had become a useful tool in the spread of the good news. His friendship with Chun had never been for political advantage, only to present and embody the gospel message. And now the gospel would be broadcast farther into North Korea.

VISITING A FORMER PRESIDENT IN PRISON

Billy was well known for frequently visiting the inmates in prisons, comforting them, and sharing the good news of the gospel with them. One person whom he had visited in the prison cells was former president Tae Woo Roh (1988–93), who was later convicted of corruption and other charges. (He would receive a presidential pardon seventeen months later.) President Roh was a devout Buddhist through the influence of his mother. However, during his prison stay, he read through the entire Old and New Testaments of the Bible, showing great interest in Christianity.

The two had first met during the Blue House worship service, during President Chung Hee Park's official term. At that time, the chief bodyguard, Mr. Ji Chul Cha, invited several pastors from various Christian denominations to lead the Blue House worship service. Billy had been invited on several occasions, and that is when former president Roh had also attended, as the assistant for the vice-chief deputy.

Later, President Roh's son and daughter, Jae Hun and So Young, began attending the youth service at the Suwon Central Baptist Church. During his presidency, Roh especially had an inclination toward North Korea. Slightly differing in purpose, Billy also had his heart set on the "North." Billy's focus was on missions through FEBC's northern broadcast, but President Roh's interest in the North was to achieve diplomatic relations between the North and South.

After official diplomatic ties had been made between the North and South, in 1992, President Roh visited China and realized how much the missionary work had contributed to the northern regional diplomacy. He had expected the long history of socialism embedded in the ethnic Korean Chinese would have inclined their hearts toward North Korea. On the contrary, when he met individually with a large number of Korean descendants there, he was surprised to find that their hearts were much inclined toward South Korea.

THE SURPRISING IMPACT OF FEBC-KOREA

One major contributing factor was FEBC-Korea. Two million ethnic Korean Chinese were yearning for the free and plentiful lifestyle of South Korea as they listened to the FEBC-Korea broadcast. FEBC-Korea's efforts in reaching the northern lands were not merely a vague resonance in their hearts. It was a much needed, refreshing spring rain of life and blessing, soaking the depth of their hearts. It was a plentiful rainbow of hope.

Immediately after his return, President Roh spoke to thirty domestic religious leaders in Korea, saying, "I was surprised at the great power of FEBC-Korea." In February of the following year, he honored Pastor Billy Jang Hwan Kim with the Order of Civil Merit Mugunghwa Medal, which is the highest decoration given to a civilian by the government of South Korea.

After Roh's reelection defeat and subsequent conviction and imprisonment, Billy visited him regularly—thirteen times. He tried to comfort the former president and always wholeheartedly prayed for him. He read the Bible to him, sharing the hope of the gospel. Roh was thankful to Billy, saying that he had always treated him the same, whether it was before he became the president or after he had become president, whether he was in office or after he had been imprisoned. He also said that even though he did not attend church, he thought a lot about Jesus. In addition, the former president mentioned that during his imprisonment, he found comfort in Billy's visits, and this became the title of his book, *I Find Peace When I Meet Him.*

Serving prisoners is following God's command. Billy simply confessed, "All I did was to obey the command." He recalls the words of Christ: "Lord, when did we see you . . . in prison and did not help you?" He will reply, "Truly, I tell you, whatever you did not do for one of the least of these, you did not do it for me" (Matthew 25:44–45 NIV).

EPILOGUE
IN LIEU OF STORIES
NOT YET TOLD . . .

Even as old as I am, it seems as though God is not done with me as miracles continue to unfold before my eyes every day. Here are just two of the more recent.

On June 22, 2010, the Korean church held a "Prayer of Peace" event for the sixtieth anniversary of the Korean War, at the Seoul World Cup Stadium in Sangam. I was asked to invite former US President George W. Bush to be our main speaker.

In a sermon in preparation for the event, I told listeners, "Nehemiah, saddened in seeing Israel suffer, kept his homeland in his heart, fasting and praying in tears. His fervent prayer of love for his nation resulted in moving God's hand. As we face the sufferings of our divided nation, just as Nehemiah considered his people's sins as his own, we must also be contrite in the same way, and confess our sins." This was the primary reason I had proposed the Prayer of Peace event.

But there was another reason. We earnestly wanted this event to trigger a renewed revival among our churches. As Korea faced the new millennium, there arose criticisms that our churches were becoming stagnant, following in the steps of the European churches, which had become ecclesiastically authoritative, and similar to the American churches, which had become commercialized. I truly hoped that this would become an occasion of awakening for churches throughout our land.

The place for the event had social and spiritual significance, the Seoul World Cup Stadium in Sangam. Here in 2002 Korea wrote a new chapter in international soccer by becoming one of the semifinalists in the World Cup games. It had been here, that same year, on April 30, that a large joint Easter service was held, for the first time in ten years. And as His messenger I declared my hope, "Korean churches must once again arise and be united." We prayed, people filled the stadium, and revival breezes began to stir. We continue to hope that Korea will once again experience ongoing spiritual revival.

On January 8, 2013, over two hundred FEBC-Korea staff, listeners, and their families joined me for a Holy Land tour. We first arrived in Jordan. There a sudden snowstorm would overrule all our plans. Instead we held a spontaneous revival service and a surprise visit to the Syrian refugee camp in Jatari, Jordan.

In the aftermath of the storm, many of us trudged through the muddy grounds, gazing upon the poorly pitched tents. The refugees' sunken faces, filled with despair and frustration, evoked for me memories of the Korean War, a time filled with poverty and hopelessness. My memories of Sergeant Carl Powers's generosity always encourage me to help others with the same kindness that was given to a small houseboy.

After our visit we promised the Jatari refugees one hundred container houses to replace the broken tents and pledged to raise $330,000 for these houses through a live broadcast back at home. Not only did we reach our goal but earned over $1.7 million, giving us the ability to construct more than four hundred container shelters. Good People, a nongovernmental organization, collaborated with FEBC-Korea to send $400,000 in daily necessities. Another Korean company also pledged to donate one thousand container shelters. I am still in awe of the mighty power of God.

When a person meets God, he or she is not contained to only a single miracle, but rather the willing servant experiences miracles every day by lying at the foot of the cross.

I pray that the Jatari camp miracle does not end with just food and shelter but that seeds of the gospel were sown into the hearts through word and deed. We pray that through our actions, refugees saw the cross and perhaps even that a young boy of inconsequential worth may rise as a great evangelist for the next generation.

I leave you with one last remark: Never ask God to simply make history but ask for miracles to unfold.

NOTES

Prologue

1. Yong Ho Kim and Jae Sung Yoo, *When a Person Meets God, Miracles Unfold* (Seoul: Nachimban Publishing, 2010).

Chapter 1: Have Faith in God

1. Although in Western countries hyphens are used for the first name, e.g., Jang-hwan, hyphens are not used in Korea and the last name is not shown first. For cultural accuracy and sensitivity, the hyphen has been removed and the second part of the name is capitalized for all Korean names.
2. "Korean War," the History Channel, http://www.history.com/topics/korean-war; "The Korean War," *The American Experience*, http://www.pbs.org/wgbh/amex/bomb/peopleevents/ pandeAMEX58.html?utm_source=tumblr&utm_medium=thisday history&utm_campaign=June+25+Korean+War.

Chapter 2: Find the Source of Faith

1. Published in 1977, Esther's book remains in print today. Esther Ahn Kim, *If I Perish* (Chicago: Moody, 1977).
2. Interview with Jerry Major, February 25, 2015. Nearly forty years later Major would visit Billy in Korea. Now a missionary with International Needs, where he helped train nationals to do ministry in their own countries, Major preached at Pastor Kim's Central Baptist Church in Suwon.
3. Interview with Jerry Thompson, February 26, 2015.

Chapter 4: Evangelize, Starting at Home

1. Today many Korean homes use electric or hot water systems to heat the floors; in rural areas cooking briquettes still send heat through flues (tunnels) under the floors. These tunnels have been covered with cement before the flooring is installed so that the house will not catch on fire. Either way, the ondol system remains the primary form of home heating in Korea.

Chapter 5: Hold a Grand Vision

1. John Pollock, *The Billy Graham Story: Evangelist to the World* (New York: Harper & Row, 1979), 55, 60.
2. Ibid., 62.
3. Ibid., 56.
4. John Pollock, *The Billy Graham Story: The Authorized Biography* (Grand Rapids: Zondervan, 2003), 122.
5. "Another Billy, Pastor Billy Kim," *Chosun*, June 3, 1973.
6. Pollock, *The Billy Graham Story: Evangelist*, 62.
7. Ibid., 64.

Chapter 6: Spread the Gospel with Your Whole Life

1. In recent years Billy Kim has contributed financially to Bob Jones University "in appreciation for the education I received there," and he has been invited to class re-

unions. Billy adds, "I think I am in good standing, since I have received an invitation to attend the homecoming for 1958 graduates."

2. "Promise Keepers '97: The Making of a Godly Man," www.promisekeepers.org/pk-history.

3. Stanley Sebastian Kresge Jr. is the son of the chairman of S. S. Kresge Company, the forerunner of Kmart.

4. An estimated 1,850 houses were destroyed and 3,000 people were either killed or injured. See James Brooke, "North Korea Appeals for Help after Railway Explosion," *New York Times*, April 24, 2004, http://www.nytimes.com/2004/04/24/world/north-korea-appeals-for-help-after-railway-explosion.html.

5. Denton Lotz, Baptist World Alliance Secretary General, and associate David Maddox assisted Kim in his mission to East Europe.

Chapter 7: Grab Hold of the God-Given Chance

1. Yong Ho Kim and Jae Sung Yoo, *When a Person Meets God, Miracles Unfold* (Seoul: Nachimban Publishing, 2010), 139.

Chapter 8: Value People and Save Money

1. Yong Ho Kim and Jae Sung Yoo, *When a Person Meets God, Miracles Unfold* (Seoul: Nachimban Publishing, 2010), 153.

Chapter 9: Manage in the Lord's Way

1. Korea had sent many of their war orphans to new homes in America and other countries. Eventually the number of orphans sent abroad became a matter of embarrassment to Korea. They began to build orphanages. Later, however, Korea looked to local adoption for the orphans.

2. In Korea, wives retain their maiden names after they marry.

Chapter 10: Marching toward a Bigger Dream

1. Billy (Jang Hwan) Kim has been awarded twenty honorary doctoral degrees—five from Korean universities and fifteen from American schools of higher education. These include the doctor of divinity (DD) from Biola University (2010) and the doctor of laws (LLD) from LeTourneau University (2003).

Chapter 11: Meet the Right Partners

1. Paul Johnson's assistance to Billy and Trudy Kim is recounted in the chapter "My Involvement with a Korean Houseboy" in his autobiography, Paul H. Johnson, *My Cup Runneth Over* (Seattle: CreateSpace/Amazon, 2013), 201–203.

Chapter 12: Serve with a Pure Heart

1. Carl L. Powers, *A Heart Speaks* (Seoul: Nachimban-Compass, 1995), 13.

2. Ibid., 14.

3. Ibid., 51.

Chapter 16: Serve for the Gospel

1. Interview with John Chancellor, *NBC Nightly News*, 1973.

FEBC KOREA *in Los Angeles*

Christ to the World by Radio

GO MATT 28:19

THEREFORE
———— & ————
MAKE DISCIPLES
OF ALL NATIONS

FEBC-Korea in Los Angeles began in 1985 to support the work of Far East Broadcasting Company-Korea (FEBC-Korea), a top-rated South Korean, Christian broadcasting network. Starting July 2012, FEBC-Korea in LA began airing its own on-air radio, adding new web content in 2014 to utilize innovative digital platforms to reach a wider global audience for Christ.

usk.febc.net • 15700 Imperial Hwy, La Mirada, CA • 562.448.1782

FEBC-Korea
Since 1956

12 Stations • 5 Languages

febc.net

FEBC International
Since 1948

52 Countries
147 Stations • 100 Languages

febc.org

A BIOGRAPHY FROM MOODY PUBLISHERS:
D. L. MOODY—A LIFE

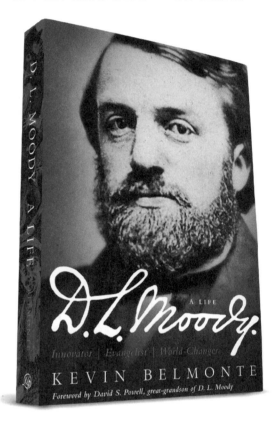

He burst on the fusty corridors of Victorian spirituality like a breath of fresh air, regaling one prime minister with his sense of humor and touching the lives of seven presidents.

Who was this man? A visionary educator and fundraiser, D. L. Moody was also a renowned evangelist in the nineteenth century. Long before radio and television, he brought the transformative message of the gospel before 100 million people on both sides of the Atlantic.

Drawing on the best, most recent scholarship, *D. L. Moody—A Life* chronicles the incredible journey of one of the great souls of history.

MOODY
Publishers™

From the Word to Life